New Poems

Robert Louis Stevenson

CONTENTS

PRAYER
LO! IN THINE HONEST EYES I READ
THOUGH DEEP INDIFFERENCE SHOULD DROWSE
MY HEART, WHEN FIRST THE BLACKBIRD SINGS
I DREAMED OF FOREST ALLEYS FAIR
ST. MARTIN'S SUMMER
DEDICATION
THE OLD CHIMAERAS, OLD RECEIPTS
PRELUDE
THE VANQUISHED KNIGHT
TO THE COMMISSIONERS OF NORTHERN LIGHTS
THE RELIC TAKEN, WHAT AVAILS THE SHRINE?
ABOUT THE SHELTERED GARDEN GROUND
AFTER READING "ANTONY AND CLEOPATRA"
I KNOW NOT HOW, BUT AS I COUNT
SPRING SONG
THE SUMMER SUN SHONE ROUND ME
YOU LOOKED SO TEMPTING IN THE PEW
LOVE'S VICISSITUDES
DUDDINGSTONE
STOUT MARCHES LEAD TO CERTAIN ENDS
AWAY WITH FUNERAL MUSIC
TO SYDNEY
HAD I THE POWER THAT HAVE THE WILL
O DULL COLD NORTHERN SKY
APOLOGETIC POSTSCRIPT OF A YEAR LATER
TO MARCUS
TO OTTILIE
THIS GLOOMY NORTHERN DAY
THE WIND IS WITHOUT THERE AND HOWLS IN THE TREES
A VALENTINE'S SONG
HAIL! CHILDISH SLAVES OF SOCIAL RULES
SWALLOWS TRAVEL TO AND FRO
TO MESDAMES ZASSETSKY AND GARSCHINE
TO MADAME GARSCHINE
MUSIC AT THE VILLA MARINA
FEAR NOT, DEAR FRIEND, BUT FREELY LIVE YOUR DAYS
LET LOVE GO, IF GO SHE WILL
I DO NOT FEAR TO OWN ME KIN
I AM LIKE ONE THAT FOR LONG DAYS HAD SATE

VOLUNTARY
ON NOW, ALTHOUGH THE YEAR BE DONE
IN THE GREEN AND GALLANT SPRING
DEATH, TO THE DEAD FOR EVERMORE
TO CHARLES BAXTER
I WHO ALL THE WINTER THROUGH
LOVE, WHAT IS LOVE?
SOON OUR FRIENDS PERISH
AS ONE WHO HAVING WANDERED ALL NIGHT LONG
STRANGE ARE THE WAYS OF MEN
THE WIND BLEW SHRILL AND SMART
MAN SAILS THE DEEP AWHILE
THE COCK'S CLEAR VOICE INTO THE CLEARER AIR
NOW WHEN THE NUMBER OF MY YEARS
WHAT MAN MAY LEARN, WHAT MAN MAY DO
SMALL IS THE TRUST WHEN LOVE IS GREEN
KNOW YOU THE RIVER NEAR TO GREZ
IT'S FORTH ACROSS THE ROARING FOAM
AN ENGLISH BREEZE
AS IN THEIR FLIGHT THE BIRDS OF SONG
THE PIPER
TO MRS. MACMARLAND
TO MISS CORNISH
TALES OF ARABIA
BEHOLD, AS GOBLINS DARK OF MIEN
STILL I LOVE TO RHYME
LONG TIME I LAY IN LITTLE EASE
FLOWER GOD, GOD OF THE SPRING
COME, MY BELOVED, HEAR FROM ME
SINCE YEARS AGO FOR EVERMORE
ENVOY FOR "A CHILD'S GARDEN OF VERSES"
FOR RICHMOND'S GARDEN WALL
HAIL, GUEST, AND ENTER FREELY!
LO, NOW, MY GUEST
SO LIVE, SO LOVE, SO USE THAT FRAGILE HOUR
AD SE IPSUM
BEFORE THIS LITTLE GIFT WAS COME
GO, LITTLE BOOK - THE ANCIENT PHRASE
MY LOVE WAS WARM
DEDICATORY POEM FOR "UNDERWOODS"
FAREWELL
THE FAR-FARERS
COME, MY LITTLE CHILDREN, HERE ARE SONGS FOR YOU

HOME FROM THE DAISIED MEADOWS
EARLY IN THE MORNING I HEAR ON YOUR PIANO
FAIR ISLE AT SEA
LOUD AND LOW IN THE CHIMNEY
I LOVE TO BE WARM BY THE RED FIRESIDE
AT LAST SHE COMES
MINE EYES WERE SWIFT TO KNOW THEE
FIXED IS THE DOOM
MEN ARE HEAVEN'S PIERS
THE ANGLER ROSE, HE TOOK HIS ROD
SPRING CAROL
TO WHAT SHALL I COMPARE HER
WHEN THE SUN COMES AFTER RAIN
LATE, O MILLER
TO FRIENDS AT HOME
I, WHOM APOLLO SOMETIME VISITED
TEMPEST TOSSED AND SORE AFFLICTED
VARIANT FORM OF THE PRECEDING POEM
I NOW, O FRIEND, WHOM NOISELESSLY THE SNOWS
SINCE THOU HAST GIVEN ME THIS GOOD HOPE, O GOD
GOD GAVE TO ME A CHILD IN PART
OVER THE LAND IS APRIL
LIGHT AS THE LINNET ON MY WAY I START
COMIC, HERE IS ADIEU TO THE CITY
IT BLOWS A SNOWING GALE
NE SIT ANCILLAE TIBI AMOR PUDOR
TO ALL THAT LOVE THE FAR AND BLUE
THOU STRAINEST THROUGH THE MOUNTAIN FERN
TO ROSABELLE
NOW BARE TO THE BEHOLDER'S EYE
THE BOUR-TREE DEN
SONNETS
FRAGMENTS
AIR OF DIABELLI'S
EPITAPHIUM EROTII
DE M. ANTONIO
AD MAGISTRUM LUDI
AD NEPOTEM
IN CHARIDEMUM
DE LIGURRA
IN LUPUM
AD QUINTILIANUM
DE HORTIS JULII MARTIALIS

AD MARTIALEM
IN MAXIMUM
AD OLUM
DE COENATIONE MICAE
DE EROTIO PUELLA
AD PISCATOREM

PRAYER

I ASK good things that I detest,
With speeches fair;
Heed not, I pray Thee, Lord, my breast,
But hear my prayer.

I say ill things I would not say -
Things unaware:
Regard my breast, Lord, in Thy day,
And not my prayer.

My heart is evil in Thy sight:
My good thoughts flee:
O Lord, I cannot wish aright -
Wish Thou for me.

O bend my words and acts to Thee,
However ill,
That I, whate'er I say or be,
May serve Thee still.

O let my thoughts abide in Thee
Lest I should fall:
Show me Thyself in all I see,
Thou Lord of all.

LO! IN THINE HONEST EYES I READ

LO! in thine honest eyes I read
The auspicious beacon that shall lead,
After long sailing in deep seas,
To quiet havens in June ease.

Thy voice sings like an inland bird
First by the seaworn sailor heard;
And like road sheltered from life's sea
Thine honest heart is unto me.

New Poems

THOUGH DEEP INDIFFERENCE SHOULD DROWSE

THOUGH deep indifference should drowse
The sluggish life beneath my brows,
And all the external things I see
Grow snow-showers in the street to me,
Yet inmost in my stormy sense
Thy looks shall be an influence.

Though other loves may come and go
And long years sever us below,
Shall the thin ice that grows above
Freeze the deep centre-well of love?
No, still below light amours, thou
Shalt rule me as thou rul'st me now.

Year following year shall only set
Fresh gems upon thy coronet;
And Time, grown lover, shall delight
To beautify thee in my sight;
And thou shalt ever rule in me
Crowned with the light of memory.

New Poems

MY HEART, WHEN FIRST THE BLACK-BIRD SINGS

MY heart, when first the blackbird sings,
My heart drinks in the song:
Cool pleasure fills my bosom through
And spreads each nerve along.

My bosom eddies quietly,
My heart is stirred and cool
As when a wind-moved briar sweeps
A stone into a pool

But unto thee, when thee I meet,
My pulses thicken fast,
As when the maddened lake grows black
And ruffles in the blast.

New Poems

I DREAMED OF FOREST ALLEYS FAIR

I.

I DREAMED of forest alleys fair
And fields of gray-flowered grass,
Where by the yellow summer moon
My Jenny seemed to pass.

I dreamed the yellow summer moon,
Behind a cedar wood,
Lay white on fields of rippling grass
Where I and Jenny stood.

I dreamed - but fallen through my dream,
In a rainy land I lie
Where wan wet morning crowns the hills
Of grim reality.

II.

I am as one that keeps awake
All night in the month of June,
That lies awake in bed to watch
The trees and great white moon.

For memories of love are more
Than the white moon there above,
And dearer than quiet moonshine
Are the thoughts of her I love.

III.

Last night I lingered long without
My last of loves to see.
Alas! the moon-white window-panes
Stared blindly back on me.

To-day I hold her very hand,
Her very waist embrace -
Like clouds across a pool, I read
Her thoughts upon her face.

And yet, as now, through her clear eyes
I seek the inner shrine -
I stoop to read her virgin heart
In doubt if it be mine -

O looking long and fondly thus,
What vision should I see?
No vision, but my own white face
That grins and mimics me.

IV.

Once more upon the same old seat
In the same sunshiny weather,
The elm-trees' shadows at their feet
And foliage move together.

The shadows shift upon the grass,
The dial point creeps on;
The clear sun shines, the loiterers pass,
As then they passed and shone.

But now deep sleep is on my heart,
Deep sleep and perfect rest.
Hope's flutterings now disturb no more
The quiet of my breast.

New Poems

ST. MARTIN'S SUMMER

AS swallows turning backward
When half-way o'er the sea,
At one word's trumpet summons
They came again to me -
The hopes I had forgotten
Came back again to me.

I know not which to credit,
O lady of my heart!
Your eyes that bade me linger,
Your words that bade us part -
I know not which to credit,
My reason or my heart.

But be my hopes rewarded,
Or be they but in vain,
I have dreamed a golden vision,
I have gathered in the grain -
I have dreamed a golden vision,
I have not lived in vain.

New Poems

DEDICATION

MY first gift and my last, to you
I dedicate this fascicle of songs -
The only wealth I have:
Just as they are, to you.

I speak the truth in soberness, and say
I had rather bring a light to your clear eyes,
Had rather hear you praise
This bosomful of songs

Than that the whole, hard world with one consent,
In one continuous chorus of applause
Poured forth for me and mine
The homage of ripe praise.

I write the finis here against my love,
This is my love's last epitaph and tomb.
Here the road forks, and I
Go my way, far from yours.

New Poems

THE OLD CHIMAERAS, OLD RECEIPTS

THE old Chimaeras, old receipts
For making "happy land,"
The old political beliefs
Swam close before my hand.

The grand old communistic myths
In a middle state of grace,
Quite dead, but not yet gone to Hell,
And walking for a space,

Quite dead, and looking it, and yet
All eagerness to show
The Social-Contract forgeries
By Chatterton - Rousseau -

A hundred such as these I tried,
And hundreds after that,
I fitted Social Theories
As one would fit a hat!

Full many a marsh-fire lured me on,
I reached at many a star,
I reached and grasped them and behold -
The stump of a cigar!

All through the sultry sweltering day
The sweat ran down my brow,
The still plains heard my distant strokes
That have been silenced now.

This way and that, now up, now down,
I hailed full many a blow.
Alas! beneath my weary arm
The thicket seemed to grow.

I take the lesson, wipe my brow
And throw my axe aside,
And, sorely wearied, I go home
In the tranquil eventide.

And soon the rising moon, that lights
The eve of my defeat,
Shall see me sitting as of yore
By my old master's feet.

PRELUDE

BY sunny market-place and street
Wherever I go my drum I beat,
And wherever I go in my coat of red
The ribbons flutter about my head.

I seek recruits for wars to come -
For slaughterless wars I beat the drum,
And the shilling I give to each new ally
Is hope to live and courage to die.

I know that new recruits shall come
Wherever I beat the sounding drum,
Till the roar of the march by country and town
Shall shake the tottering Dagons down.

For I was objectless as they
And loitering idly day by day;
But whenever I heard the recruiters come,
I left my all to follow the drum.

THE VANQUISHED KNIGHT

I HAVE left all upon the shameful field,
Honour and Hope, my God, and all but life;
Spurless, with sword reversed and dinted shield,
Degraded and disgraced, I leave the strife.

From him that hath not, shall there not be taken
E'en that he hath, when he deserts the strife?
Life left by all life's benefits forsaken,
O keep the promise, Lord, and take the life.

TO THE COMMISSIONERS OF NORTHERN LIGHTS

I SEND to you, commissioners,
A paper that may please ye, sirs
(For troth they say it might be worse
An' I believe't)
And on your business lay my curse
Before I leav't.

I thocht I'd serve wi' you, sirs, yince,
But I've thocht better of it since;
The maitter I will nowise mince,
But tell ye true:
I'll service wi' some ither prince,
An' no wi' you.

I've no been very deep, ye'll think,
Cam' delicately to the brink
An' when the water gart me shrink
Straucht took the rue,
An' didna stoop my fill to drink -
I own it true.

I kent on cape and isle, a light
Burnt fair an' clearly ilka night;
But at the service I took fright,
As sune's I saw,
An' being still a neophite
Gaed straucht awa'.

Anither course I now begin,
The weeg I'll cairry for my sin,
The court my voice shall echo in,
An' - wha can tell? -
Some ither day I may be yin
O' you mysel'.

THE RELIC TAKEN, WHAT AVAILS THE SHRINE?

THE relic taken, what avails the shrine?
The locket, pictureless? O heart of mine,
Art thou not worse than that,
Still warm, a vacant nest where love once sat?

Her image nestled closer at my heart
Than cherished memories, healed every smart
And warmed it more than wine
Or the full summer sun in noon-day shine.

This was the little weather gleam that lit
The cloudy promontories - the real charm was
That gilded hills and woods
And walked beside me thro' the solitudes.

The sun is set. My heart is widowed now
Of that companion-thought. Alone I plough
The seas of life, and trace
A separate furrow far from her and grace.

New Poems

ABOUT THE SHELTERED GARDEN GROUND

ABOUT the sheltered garden ground
The trees stand strangely still.
The vale ne'er seemed so deep before,
Nor yet so high the hill.

An awful sense of quietness,
A fulness of repose,
Breathes from the dewy garden-lawns,
The silent garden rows.

As the hoof-beats of a troop of horse
Heard far across a plain,
A nearer knowledge of great thoughts
Thrills vaguely through my brain.

I lean my head upon my arm,
My heart's too full to think;
Like the roar of seas, upon my heart
Doth the morning stillness sink.

New Poems

AFTER READING "ANTONY AND CLEOPATRA"

AS when the hunt by holt and field
Drives on with horn and strife,
Hunger of hopeless things pursues
Our spirits throughout life.

The sea's roar fills us aching full
Of objectless desire -
The sea's roar, and the white moon-shine,
And the reddening of the fire.

Who talks to me of reason now?
It would be more delight
To have died in Cleopatra's arms
Than be alive to-night.

New Poems

I KNOW NOT HOW, BUT AS I COUNT

I KNOW not how, but as I count
The beads of former years,
Old laughter catches in my throat
With the very feel of tears.

SPRING SONG

THE air was full of sun and birds,
The fresh air sparkled clearly.
Remembrance wakened in my heart
And I knew I loved her dearly.

The fallows and the leafless trees
And all my spirit tingled.
My earliest thought of love, and Spring's
First puff of perfume mingled.

In my still heart the thoughts awoke,
Came lone by lone together -
Say, birds and Sun and Spring, is Love
A mere affair of weather?

New Poems

THE SUMMER SUN SHONE ROUND ME

THE summer sun shone round me,
The folded valley lay
In a stream of sun and odour,
That sultry summer day.

The tall trees stood in the sunlight
As still as still could be,
But the deep grass sighed and rustled
And bowed and beckoned me.

The deep grass moved and whispered
And bowed and brushed my face.
It whispered in the sunshine:
"The winter comes apace. "

YOU LOOKED SO TEMPTING IN THE PEW

YOU looked so tempting in the pew,
You looked so sly and calm -
My trembling fingers played with yours
As both looked out the Psalm.

Your heart beat hard against my arm,
My foot to yours was set,
Your loosened ringlet burned my cheek
Whenever they two met.

O little, little we hearkened, dear,
And little, little cared,
Although the parson sermonised,
The congregation stared.

New Poems

LOVE'S VICISSITUDES

AS Love and Hope together
Walk by me for a while,
Link-armed the ways they travel
For many a pleasant mile -
Link-armed and dumb they travel,
They sing not, but they smile.

Hope leaving, Love commences
To practise on the lute;
And as he sings and travels
With lingering, laggard foot,
Despair plays obligato
The sentimental flute.

Until in singing garments
Comes royally, at call -
Comes limber-hipped Indiff'rence
Free stepping, straight and tall -
Comes singing and lamenting,
The sweetest pipe of all.

New Poems

DUDDINGSTONE

WITH caws and chirrupings, the woods
In this thin sun rejoice.
The Psalm seems but the little kirk
That sings with its own voice.

The cloud-rifts share their amber light
With the surface of the mere -
I think the very stones are glad
To feel each other near.

Once more my whole heart leaps and swells
And gushes o'er with glee;
The fingers of the sun and shade
Touch music stops in me.

Now fancy paints that bygone day
When you were here, my fair -
The whole lake rang with rapid skates
In the windless winter air.

You leaned to me, I leaned to you,
Our course was smooth as flight -
We steered - a heel-touch to the left,
A heel-touch to the right.

We swung our way through flying men,
Your hand lay fast in mine:
We saw the shifting crowd dispart,
The level ice-reach shine.

I swear by yon swan-travelled lake,
By yon calm hill above,
I swear had we been drowned that day
We had been drowned in love.

New Poems

STOUT MARCHES LEAD TO CERTAIN ENDS

STOUT marches lead to certain ends,
We seek no Holy Grail, my friends -
That dawn should find us every day
Some fraction farther on our way.

The dumb lands sleep from east to west,
They stretch and turn and take their rest.
The cock has crown in the steading-yard,
But priest and people slumber hard.

We two are early forth, and hear
The nations snoring far and near.
So peacefully their rest they take,
It seems we are the first awake!

- Strong heart! this is no royal way,
A thousand cross-roads seek the day;
And, hid from us, to left and right,
A thousand seekers seek the light.

New Poems

AWAY WITH FUNERAL MUSIC

AWAY with funeral music - set
The pipe to powerful lips -
The cup of life's for him that drinks
And not for him that sips.

New Poems

TO SYDNEY

NOT thine where marble-still and white
Old statues share the tempered light
And mock the uneven modern flight,
But in the stream
Of daily sorrow and delight
To seek a theme.

I too, O friend, have steeled my heart
Boldly to choose the better part,
To leave the beaten ways of art,
And wholly free
To dare, beyond the scanty chart,
The deeper sea.

All vain restrictions left behind,
Frail bark! I loose my anchored mind
And large, before the prosperous wind
Desert the strand -
A new Columbus sworn to find
The morning land.

Nor too ambitious, friend. To thee
I own my weakness. Not for me
To sing the enfranchised nations' glee,
Or count the cost
Of warships foundered far at sea
And battles lost.

High on the far-seen, sunny hills,
Morning-content my bosom fills;
Well-pleased, I trace the wandering rills
And learn their birth.
Far off, the clash of sovereign wills
May shake the earth.

The nimble circuit of the wheel,
The uncertain poise of merchant weal,
Heaven of famine, fire and steel
When nations fall;

These, heedful, from afar I feel -
I mark them all.

But not, my friend, not these I sing,
My voice shall fill a narrower ring.
Tired souls, that flag upon the wing,
I seek to cheer:
Brave wines to strengthen hope I bring,
Life's cantineer!

Some song that shall be suppling oil
To weary muscles strained with toil,
Shall hearten for the daily moil,
Or widely read
Make sweet for him that tills the soil
His daily bread.

Such songs in my flushed hours I dream
(High thought) instead of armour gleam
Or warrior cantos ream by ream
To load the shelves -
Songs with a lilt of words, that seem
To sing themselves.

New Poems

HAD I THE POWER THAT HAVE THE WILL

HAD I the power that have the will,
The enfeebled will - a modern curse -
This book of mine should blossom still
A perfect garden-ground of verse.

White placid marble gods should keep
Good watch in every shadowy lawn;
And from clean, easy-breathing sleep
The birds should waken me at dawn.

- A fairy garden; - none the less
Throughout these gracious paths of mine
All day there should be free access
For stricken hearts and lives that pine;

And by the folded lawns all day -
No idle gods for such a land -
All active Love should take its way
With active Labour hand in hand.

O DULL COLD NORTHERN SKY

O DULL cold northern sky,
O brawling sabbath bells,
O feebly twittering Autumn bird that tells
The year is like to die!

O still, spoiled trees, O city ways,
O sun desired in vain,
O dread presentiment of coming rain
That cloys the sullen days!

Thee, heart of mine, I greet.
In what hard mountain pass
Striv'st thou? In what importunate morass
Sink now thy weary feet?

Thou run'st a hopeless race
To win despair. No crown
Awaits success, but leaden gods look down
On thee, with evil face.

And those that would befriend
And cherish thy defeat,
With angry welcome shall turn sour the sweet
Home-coming of the end.

Yea, those that offer praise
To idleness, shall yet
Insult thee, coming glorious in the sweat
Of honourable ways.

New Poems

APOLOGETIC POSTSCRIPT OF A YEAR LATER

IF you see this song, my dear,
And last year's toast,
I'm confoundedly in fear
You'll be serious and severe
About the boast.

Blame not that I sought such aid
To cure regret.
I was then so lowly laid
I used all the Gasconnade
That I could get.

Being snubbed is somewhat smart,
Believe, my sweet;
And I needed all my art
To restore my broken heart
To its conceit.

Come and smile, dear, and forget
I boasted so,
I apologise - regret -
It was all a jest; - and - yet -
I do not know.

New Poems

TO MARCUS

YOU have been far, and I
Been farther yet,
Since last, in foul or fair
An impecunious pair,
Below this northern sky
Of ours, we met.

Now winter night shall see
Again us two,
While howls the tempest higher,
Sit warmly by the fire
And dream and plan, as we
Were wont to do.

And, hand in hand, at large
Our thoughts shall walk
While storm and gusty rain,
Again and yet again,
Shall drive their noisy charge
Across the talk.

The pleasant future still
Shall smile to me,
And hope with wooing hands
Wave on to fairy lands
All over dale and hill
And earth and sea.

And you who doubt the sky
And fear the sun -
You - Christian with the pack -
You shall not wander back
For I am Hopeful - I
Will cheer you on.

Come - where the great have trod,
The great shall lead -
Come, elbow through the press,
Pluck Fortune by the dress -

New Poems

By God, we must - by God,
We shall succeed.

TO OTTILIE

YOU remember, I suppose,
How the August sun arose,
And how his face
Woke to trill and carolette
All the cages that were set
About the place.

In the tender morning light
All around lay strange and bright
And still and sweet,
And the gray doves unafraid
Went their morning promenade
Along the street.

THIS GLOOMY NORTHERN DAY

THIS gloomy northern day,
Or this yet gloomier night,
Has moved a something high
In my cold heart; and I,
That do not often pray,
Would pray to-night.

And first on Thee I call
For bread, O God of might!
Enough of bread for all, -
That through the famished town
Cold hunger may lie down
With none to-night.

I pray for hope no less,
Strong-sinewed hope, O Lord,
That to the struggling young
May preach with brazen tongue
Stout Labour, high success,
And bright reward.

And last, O Lord, I pray
For hearts resigned and bold
To trudge the dusty way -
Hearts stored with song and joke
And warmer than a cloak
Against the cold.

If nothing else he had,
He who has this, has all.
This comforts under pain;
This, through the stinging rain,
Keeps ragamuffin glad
Behind the wall.

This makes the sanded inn
A palace for a Prince,
And this, when griefs begin
And cruel fate annoys,

Can bring to mind the joys
Of ages since.

New Poems

THE WIND IS WITHOUT THERE AND HOWLS IN THE TREES

THE wind is without there and howls in the trees,
And the rain-flurries drum on the glass:
Alone by the fireside with elbows on knees
I can number the hours as they pass.
Yet now, when to cheer me the crickets begin,
And my pipe is just happily lit,
Believe me, my friend, tho' the evening draws in,
That not all uncontested I sit.

Alone, did I say? O no, nowise alone
With the Past sitting warm on my knee,
To gossip of days that are over and gone,
But still charming to her and to me.
With much to be glad of and much to deplore,
Yet, as these days with those we compare,
Believe me, my friend, tho' the sorrows seem more
They are somehow more easy to bear.

And thou, faded Future, uncertain and frail,
As I cherish thy light in each draught,
His lamp is not more to the miner - their sail
Is not more to the crew on the raft.
For Hope can make feeble ones earnest and brave,
And, as forth thro' the years I look on,
Believe me, my friend, between this and the grave,
I see wonderful things to be done.

To do or to try; and, believe me, my friend,
If the call should come early for me,
I can leave these foundations uprooted, and tend
For some new city over the sea.
To do or to try; and if failure be mine,
And if Fortune go cross to my plan,
Believe me, my friend, tho' I mourn the design
I shall never lament for the man.

A VALENTINE'S SONG

MOTLEY I count the only wear
That suits, in this mixed world, the truly wise,
Who boldly smile upon despair
And shake their bells in Grandam Grundy's eyes.
Singers should sing with such a goodly cheer
That the bare listening should make strong like wine,
At this unruly time of year,
The Feast of Valentine.

We do not now parade our "oughts"
And "shoulds" and motives and beliefs in God.
Their life lies all indoors; sad thoughts
Must keep the house, while gay thoughts go abroad,
Within we hold the wake for hopes deceased;
But in the public streets, in wind or sun,
Keep open, at the annual feast,
The puppet-booth of fun.

Our powers, perhaps, are small to please,
But even negro-songs and castanettes,
Old jokes and hackneyed repartees
Are more than the parade of vain regrets.
Let Jacques stand Wert(h)ering by the wounded deer -
We shall make merry, honest friends of mine,
At this unruly time of year,
The Feast of Valentine.

I know how, day by weary day,
Hope fades, love fades, a thousand pleasures fade.
I have not trudged in vain that way
On which life's daylight darkens, shade by shade.
And still, with hopes decreasing, griefs increased,
Still, with what wit I have shall I, for one,
Keep open, at the annual feast,
The puppet-booth of fun.

I care not if the wit be poor,
The old worn motley stained with rain and tears,
If but the courage still endure

That filled and strengthened hope in earlier years;
If still, with friends averted, fate severe,
A glad, untainted cheerfulness be mine
To greet the unruly time of year,
The Feast of Valentine.

Priest, I am none of thine, and see
In the perspective of still hopeful youth
That Truth shall triumph over thee -
Truth to one's self - I know no other truth.
I see strange days for thee and thine, O priest,
And how your doctrines, fallen one by one,
Shall furnish at the annual feast
The puppet-booth of fun.

Stand on your putrid ruins - stand,
White neck-clothed bigot, fixedly the same,
Cruel with all things but the hand,
Inquisitor in all things but the name.
Back, minister of Christ and source of fear -
We cherish freedom - back with thee and thine
From this unruly time of year,
The Feast of Valentine.

Blood thou mayest spare; but what of tears?
But what of riven households, broken faith -
Bywords that cling through all men's years
And drag them surely down to shame and death?
Stand back, O cruel man, O foe of youth,
And let such men as hearken not thy voice
Press freely up the road to truth,
The King's highway of choice.

New Poems

HAIL! CHILDISH SLAVES OF SOCIAL RULES

HAIL! Childish slaves of social rules
You had yourselves a hand in making!
How I could shake your faith, ye fools,
If but I thought it worth the shaking.
I see, and pity you; and then
Go, casting off the idle pity,
In search of better, braver men,
My own way freely through the city.

My own way freely, and not yours;
And, careless of a town's abusing,
Seek real friendship that endures
Among the friends of my own choosing.
I'll choose my friends myself, do you hear?
And won't let Mrs. Grundy do it,
Tho' all I honour and hold dear
And all I hope should move me to it.

I take my old coat from the shelf -
I am a man of little breeding.
And only dress to please myself -
I own, a very strange proceeding.
I smoke a pipe abroad, because
To all cigars I much prefer it,
And as I scorn your social laws
My choice has nothing to deter it.

Gladly I trudge the footpath way,
While you and yours roll by in coaches
In all the pride of fine array,
Through all the city's thronged approaches.
O fine religious, decent folk,
In Virtue's flaunting gold and scarlet,
I sneer between two puffs of smoke, -
Give me the publican and harlot.

Ye dainty-spoken, stiff, severe
Seed of the migrated Philistian,
One whispered question in your ear -

Pray, what was Christ, if you be Christian?
If Christ were only here just now,
Among the city's wynds and gables
Teaching the life he taught us, how
Would he be welcome to your tables?

I go and leave your logic-straws,
Your former-friends with face averted,
Your petty ways and narrow laws,
Your Grundy and your God, deserted.
From your frail ark of lies, I flee
I know not where, like Noah's raven.
Full to the broad, unsounded sea
I swim from your dishonest haven.

Alone on that unsounded deep,
Poor waif, it may be I shall perish,
Far from the course I thought to keep,
Far from the friends I hoped to cherish.
It may be that I shall sink, and yet
Hear, thro' all taunt and scornful laughter,
Through all defeat and all regret,
The stronger swimmers coming after.

SWALLOWS TRAVEL TO AND FRO

SWALLOWS travel to and fro,
And the great winds come and go,
And the steady breezes blow,
Bearing perfume, bearing love.
Breezes hasten, swallows fly,
Towered clouds forever ply,
And at noonday, you and I
See the same sunshine above.

Dew and rain fall everywhere,
Harvests ripen, flowers are fair,
And the whole round earth is bare
To the moonshine and the sun;
And the live air, fanned with wings,
Bright with breeze and sunshine, brings
Into contact distant things,
And makes all the countries one.

Let us wander where we will,
Something kindred greets us still;
Something seen on vale or hill
Falls familiar on the heart;
So, at scent or sound or sight,
Severed souls by day and night
Tremble with the same delight -
Tremble, half the world apart.

New Poems

TO MESDAMES ZASSETSKY AND GARSCHINE

THE wind may blaw the lee-gang way
And aye the lift be mirk an' gray,
An deep the moss and steigh the brae
Where a' maun gang -
There's still an hoor in ilka day
For luve and sang.

And canty hearts are strangely steeled.
By some dikeside they'll find a bield,
Some couthy neuk by muir or field
They're sure to hit,
Where, frae the blatherin' wind concealed,
They'll rest a bit.

An' weel for them if kindly fate
Send ower the hills to them a mate;
They'll crack a while o' kirk an' State,
O' yowes an' rain:
An' when it's time to take the gate,
Tak' ilk his ain.

- Sic neuk beside the southern sea
I soucht - sic place o' quiet lee
Frae a' the winds o' life. To me,
Fate, rarely fair,
Had set a freendly company
To meet me there.

Kindly by them they gart me sit,
An' blythe was I to bide a bit.
Licht as o' some hame fireside lit
My life for me.
- Ower early maun I rise an' quit
This happy lee.

TO MADAME GARSCHINE

WHAT is the face, the fairest face, till Care,
Till Care the graver - Care with cunning hand,
Etches content thereon and makes it fair,
Or constancy, and love, and makes it grand?

MUSIC AT THE VILLA MARINA

FOR some abiding central source of power,
Strong-smitten steady chords, ye seem to flow
And, flowing, carry virtue. Far below,
The vain tumultuous passions of the hour
Fleet fast and disappear; and as the sun
Shines on the wake of tempests, there is cast
O'er all the shattered ruins of my past
A strong contentment as of battles won.

And yet I cry in anguish, as I hear
The long drawn pageant of your passage roll
Magnificently forth into the night.
To yon fair land ye come from, to yon sphere
Of strength and love where now ye shape your flight,
O even wings of music, bear my soul!

Ye have the power, if but ye had the will,
Strong-smitten steady chords in sequence grand,
To bear me forth into that tranquil land
Where good is no more ravelled up with ill;
Where she and I, remote upon some hill
Or by some quiet river's windless strand,
May live, and love, and wander hand in hand,
And follow nature simply, and be still.

From this grim world, where, sadly, prisoned, we
Sit bound with others' heart-strings as with chains,
And, if one moves, all suffer, - to that Goal,
If such a land, if such a sphere, there be,
Thither, from life and all life's joys and pains,
O even wings of music, bear my soul!

FEAR NOT, DEAR FRIEND, BUT FREELY LIVE YOUR DAYS

FEAR not, dear friend, but freely live your days
Though lesser lives should suffer. Such am I,
A lesser life, that what is his of sky
Gladly would give for you, and what of praise.
Step, without trouble, down the sunlit ways.
We that have touched your raiment, are made whole
From all the selfish cankers of man's soul,
And we would see you happy, dear, or die.
Therefore be brave, and therefore, dear, be free;
Try all things resolutely, till the best,
Out of all lesser betters, you shall find;
And we, who have learned greatness from you, we,
Your lovers, with a still, contented mind,
See you well anchored in some port of rest.

LET LOVE GO, IF GO SHE WILL

LET love go, if go she will.
Seek not, O fool, her wanton flight to stay.
Of all she gives and takes away
The best remains behind her still.

The best remains behind; in vain
Joy she may give and take again,
Joy she may take and leave us pain,
If yet she leave behind
The constant mind
To meet all fortunes nobly, to endure
All things with a good heart, and still be pure,
Still to be foremost in the foremost cause,
And still be worthy of the love that was.
Love coming is omnipotent indeed,
But not Love going. Let her go. The seed
Springs in the favouring Summer air, and grows,
And waxes strong; and when the Summer goes,
Remains, a perfect tree.

Joy she may give and take again,
Joy she may take and leave us pain.
O Love, and what care we?
For one thing thou hast given, O Love, one thing
Is ours that nothing can remove;
And as the King discrowned is still a King,
The unhappy lover still preserves his love.

I DO NOT FEAR TO OWN ME KIN

I DO not fear to own me kin
To the glad clods in which spring flowers begin;
Or to my brothers, the great trees,
That speak with pleasant voices in the breeze,
Loud talkers with the winds that pass;
Or to my sister, the deep grass.

Of such I am, of such my body is,
That thrills to reach its lips to kiss.
That gives and takes with wind and sun and rain
And feels keen pleasure to the point of pain.

Of such are these,
The brotherhood of stalwart trees,
The humble family of flowers,
That make a light of shadowy bowers
Or star the edges of the bent:
They give and take sweet colour and sweet scent;
They joy to shed themselves abroad;
And tree and flower and grass and sod
Thrill and leap and live and sing
With silent voices in the Spring.

Hence I not fear to yield my breath,
Since all is still unchanged by death;
Since in some pleasant valley I may be,
Clod beside clod, or tree by tree,
Long ages hence, with her I love this hour;
And feel a lively joy to share
With her the sun and rain and air,
To taste her quiet neighbourhood
As the dumb things of field and wood,
The clod, the tree, and starry flower,
Alone of all things have the power.

New Poems

I AM LIKE ONE THAT FOR LONG DAYS HAD SATE

I AM like one that for long days had sate,
With seaward eyes set keen against the gale,
On some lone foreland, watching sail by sail,
The portbound ships for one ship that was late;
And sail by sail, his heart burned up with joy,
And cruelly was quenched, until at last
One ship, the looked-for pennant at its mast,
Bore gaily, and dropt safely past the buoy;
And lo! the loved one was not there - was dead.
Then would he watch no more; no more the sea
With myriad vessels, sail by sail, perplex
His eyes and mock his longing. Weary head,
Take now thy rest; eyes, close; for no more me
Shall hopes untried elate, or ruined vex.

For thus on love I waited; thus for love
Strained all my senses eagerly and long;
Thus for her coming ever trimmed my song;
Till in the far skies coloured as a dove,
A bird gold-coloured flickered far and fled
Over the pathless waterwaste for me;
And with spread hands I watched the bright bird flee
And waited, till before me she dropped dead.
O golden bird in these dove-coloured skies
How long I sought, how long with wearied eyes
I sought, O bird, the promise of thy flight!
And now the morn has dawned, the morn has died,
The day has come and gone; and once more night
About my lone life settles, wild and wide.

VOLUNTARY

HERE in the quiet eve
My thankful eyes receive
The quiet light.
I see the trees stand fair
Against the faded air,
And star by star prepare
The perfect night.

And in my bosom, lo!
Content and quiet grow
Toward perfect peace.
And now when day is done,
Brief day of wind and sun,
The pure stars, one by one,
Their troop increase.

Keen pleasure and keen grief
Give place to great relief:
Farewell my tears!
Still sounds toward me float;
I hear the bird's small note,
Sheep from the far sheepcote,
And lowing steers.

For lo! the war is done,
Lo, now the battle won,
The trumpets still.
The shepherd's slender strain,
The country sounds again
Awake in wood and plain,
On haugh and hill.

Loud wars and loud loves cease.
I welcome my release;
And hail once more
Free foot and way world-wide.
And oft at eventide
Light love to talk beside
The hostel door.

ON NOW, ALTHOUGH THE YEAR BE DONE

ON now, although the year be done,
Now, although the love be dead,
Dead and gone;
Hear me, O loved and cherished one,
Give me still the hand that led,
Led me on.

IN THE GREEN AND GALLANT SPRING

IN the green and gallant Spring,
Love and the lyre I thought to sing,
And kisses sweet to give and take
By the flowery hawthorn brake.

Now is russet Autumn here,
Death and the grave and winter drear,
And I must ponder here aloof
While the rain is on the roof.

DEATH, TO THE DEAD FOR EVERMORE

DEATH, to the dead for evermore
A King, a God, the last, the best of friends -
Whene'er this mortal journey ends
Death, like a host, comes smiling to the door;
Smiling, he greets us, on that tranquil shore
Where neither piping bird nor peeping dawn
Disturbs the eternal sleep,
But in the stillness far withdrawn
Our dreamless rest for evermore we keep.

For as from open windows forth we peep
Upon the night-time star beset
And with dews for ever wet;
So from this garish life the spirit peers;
And lo! as a sleeping city death outspread,
Where breathe the sleepers evenly; and lo!
After the loud wars, triumphs, trumpets, tears
And clamour of man's passion, Death appears,
And we must rise and go.

Soon are eyes tired with sunshine; soon the ears
Weary of utterance, seeing all is said;
Soon, racked by hopes and fears,
The all-pondering, all-contriving head,
Weary with all things, wearies of the years;
And our sad spirits turn toward the dead;
And the tired child, the body, longs for bed.

New Poems

TO CHARLES BAXTER

ON THE DEATH OF THEIR COMMON FRIEND, MR. JOHN ADAM, CLERK OF COURT.

OUR Johnie's deid. The mair's the pity!
He's deid, an' deid o' Aqua-vitae.
O Embro', you're a shrunken city,
Noo Johnie's deid!
Tak hands, an' sing a burial ditty
Ower Johnie's heid.

To see him was baith drink an' meat,
Gaun linkin' glegly up the street.
He but to rin or tak a seat,
The wee bit body!
Bein' aye unsicken on his feet
Wi' whusky toddy.

To be aye tosh was Johnie's whim,
There's nane was better teut than him,
Though whiles his gravit-knot wad clim'
Ahint his ear,
An' whiles he'd buttons oot or in
The less ae mair.

His hair a' lang about his bree,
His tap-lip lang by inches three -
A slockened sort 'mon, ' to pree
A' sensuality -
A droutly glint was in his e'e
An' personality.

An' day an' nicht, frae daw to daw,
Dink an' perjink an' doucely braw,
Wi' a kind o' Gospel ower a',
May or October,
Like Peden, followin' the Law
An' no that sober.

Whusky an' he were pack thegether.

Whate'er the hour, whate'er the weather,
John kept himsel' wi' mistened leather
An' kindled spunk.
Wi' him, there was nae askin' whether -
John was aye drunk.

The auncient heroes gash an' bauld
In the uncanny days of auld,
The task ance fo(u)nd to which th'were called,
Stack stenchly to it.
His life sic noble lives recalled,
Little's he knew it.

Single an' straucht, he went his way.
He kept the faith an' played the play.
Whusky an' he were man an' may
Whate'er betided.
Bonny in life - in death - this twae
Were no' divided.

An' wow! but John was unco sport.
Whiles he wad smile about the Court
Malvolio-like - whiles snore an' snort
Was heard afar.
The idle winter lads' resort
Was aye John's bar.

What's merely humorous or bonny
The Worl' regairds wi' cauld astony.
Drunk men tak' aye mair place than ony;
An' sae, ye see,
The gate was aye ower thrang for Johnie -
Or you an' me.

John micht hae jingled cap an' bells,
Been a braw fule in silks an' pells,
In ane o' the auld worl's canty hells
Paris or Sodom.
I wadnae had him naething else
But Johnie Adam.

He suffered - as have a' that wan
Eternal memory frae man,

Since e'er the weary worl' began -
Mister or Madam,
Keats or Scots Burns, the Spanish Don
Or Johnie Adam.

We leuch, an' Johnie deid. An' fegs!
Hoo he had keept his stoiterin' legs
Sae lang's he did's a fact that begs
An explanation.
He stachers fifty years - syne plegs
To's destination.

New Poems

I WHO ALL THE WINTER THROUGH

I WHO all the winter through
Cherished other loves than you,
And kept hands with hoary policy in marriage-bed and pew;
Now I know the false and true,
For the earnest sun looks through,
And my old love comes to meet me in the dawning and the dew.

Now the hedged meads renew
Rustic odour, smiling hue,
And the clean air shines and tinkles as the world goes wheeling through;
And my heart springs up anew,
Bright and confident and true,
And my old love comes to meet me in the dawning and the dew.

New Poems

LOVE, WHAT IS LOVE?

LOVE - what is love? A great and aching heart;
Wrung hands; and silence; and a long despair.
Life - what is life? Upon a moorland bare
To see love coming and see love depart.

SOON OUR FRIENDS PERISH

SOON our friends perish,
Soon all we cherish
Fades as days darken - goes as flowers go.
Soon in December
Over an ember,
Lonely we hearken, as loud winds blow.

AS ONE WHO HAVING WANDERED ALL NIGHT LONG

AS one who having wandered all night long
In a perplexed forest, comes at length
In the first hours, about the matin song,
And when the sun uprises in his strength,
To the fringed margin of the wood, and sees,
Gazing afar before him, many a mile
Of falling country, many fields and trees,
And cities and bright streams and far-off Ocean's smile:

I, O Melampus, halting, stand at gaze:
I, liberated, look abroad on life,
Love, and distress, and dusty travelling ways,
The steersman's helm, the surgeon's helpful knife,
On the lone ploughman's earth-upturning share,
The revelry of cities and the sound
Of seas, and mountain-tops aloof in air,
And of the circling earth the unsupported round:

I, looking, wonder: I, intent, adore;
And, O Melampus, reaching forth my hands
In adoration, cry aloud and soar
In spirit, high above the supine lands
And the low caves of mortal things, and flee
To the last fields of the universe untrod,
Where is no man, nor any earth, nor sea,
And the contented soul is all alone with God.

STRANGE ARE THE WAYS OF MEN

STRANGE are the ways of men,
And strange the ways of God!
We tread the mazy paths
That all our fathers trod.

We tread them undismayed,
And undismayed behold
The portents of the sky,
The things that were of old.

The fiery stars pursue
Their course in heav'n on high;
And round the 'leaguered town,
Crest-tossing heroes cry.

Crest-tossing heroes cry;
And martial fifes declare
How small, to mortal minds,
Is merely mortal care.

And to the clang of steel
And cry of piercing flute
Upon the azure peaks
A God shall plant his foot:

A God in arms shall stand,
And seeing wide and far
The green and golden earth,
The killing tide of war,

He, with uplifted arm,
Shall to the skies proclaim
The gleeful fate of man,
The noble road to fame!

THE WIND BLEW SHRILL AND SMART

THE wind blew shrill and smart,
And the wind awoke my heart
Again to go a-sailing o'er the sea,
To hear the cordage moan
And the straining timbers groan,
And to see the flying pennon lie a-lee.

O sailor of the fleet,
It is time to stir the feet!
It's time to man the dingy and to row!
It's lay your hand in mine
And it's empty down the wine,
And it's drain a health to death before we go!

To death, my lads, we sail;
And it's death that blows the gale
And death that holds the tiller as we ride.
For he's the king of all
In the tempest and the squall,
And the ruler of the Ocean wild and wide!

MAN SAILS THE DEEP AWHILE

MAN sails the deep awhile;
Loud runs the roaring tide;
The seas are wild and wide;
O'er many a salt, o'er many a desert mile,
The unchained breakers ride,
The quivering stars beguile.

Hope bears the sole command;
Hope, with unshaken eyes,
Sees flaw and storm arise;
Hope, the good steersman, with unwearying hand,
Steers, under changing skies,
Unchanged toward the land.

O wind that bravely blows!
O hope that sails with all
Where stars and voices call!
O ship undaunted that forever goes
Where God, her admiral,
His battle signal shows!

What though the seas and wind
Far on the deep should whelm
Colours and sails and helm?
There, too, you touch that port that you designed -
There, in the mid-seas' realm,
Shall you that haven find.

Well hast thou sailed: now die,
To die is not to sleep.
Still your true course you keep,
O sailor soul, still sailing for the sky;
And fifty fathom deep
Your colours still shall fly.

New Poems

THE COCK'S CLEAR VOICE INTO THE CLEARER AIR

THE cock's clear voice into the clearer air
Where westward far I roam,
Mounts with a thrill of hope,
Falls with a sigh of home.

A rural sentry, he from farm and field
The coming morn descries,
And, mankind's bugler, wakes
The camp of enterprise.

He sings the morn upon the westward hills
Strange and remote and wild;
He sings it in the land
Where once I was a child.

He brings to me dear voices of the past,
The old land and the years:
My father calls for me,
My weeping spirit hears.

Fife, fife, into the golden air, O bird,
And sing the morning in;
For the old days are past
And new days begin.

New Poems

NOW WHEN THE NUMBER OF MY YEARS

NOW when the number of my years
Is all fulfilled, and I
From sedentary life
Shall rouse me up to die,
Bury me low and let me lie
Under the wide and starry sky.
Joying to live, I joyed to die,
Bury me low and let me lie.

Clear was my soul, my deeds were free,
Honour was called my name,
I fell not back from fear
Nor followed after fame.
Bury me low and let me lie
Under the wide and starry sky.
Joying to live, I joyed to die,
Bury me low and let me lie.

Bury me low in valleys green
And where the milder breeze
Blows fresh along the stream,
Sings roundly in the trees -
Bury me low and let me lie
Under the wide and starry sky.
Joying to live, I joyed to die,
Bury me low and let me lie.

WHAT MAN MAY LEARN, WHAT MAN MAY DO

WHAT man may learn, what man may do,
Of right or wrong of false or true,
While, skipper-like, his course he steers
Through nine and twenty mingled years,
Half misconceived and half forgot,
So much I know and practise not.

Old are the words of wisdom, old
The counsels of the wise and bold:
To close the ears, to check the tongue,
To keep the pining spirit young;
To act the right, to say the true,
And to be kind whate'er you do.

Thus we across the modern stage
Follow the wise of every age;
And, as oaks grow and rivers run
Unchanged in the unchanging sun,
So the eternal march of man
Goes forth on an eternal plan.

New Poems

SMALL IS THE TRUST WHEN LOVE IS GREEN

SMALL is the trust when love is green
In sap of early years;
A little thing steps in between
And kisses turn to tears.

Awhile - and see how love be grown
In loveliness and power!
Awhile, it loves the sweets alone,
But next it loves the sour.

A little love is none at all
That wanders or that fears;
A hearty love dwells still at call
To kisses or to tears.

Such then be mine, my love to give,
And such be yours to take: -
A faith to hold, a life to live,
For lovingkindness' sake:

Should you be sad, should you be gay,
Or should you prove unkind,
A love to hold the growing way
And keep the helping mind: -

A love to turn the laugh on care
When wrinkled care appears,
And, with an equal will, to share
Your losses and your tears.

KNOW YOU THE RIVER NEAR TO GREZ

KNOW you the river near to Grez,
A river deep and clear?
Among the lilies all the way,
That ancient river runs to-day
From snowy weir to weir.

Old as the Rhine of great renown,
She hurries clear and fast,
She runs amain by field and town
From south to north, from up to down,
To present on from past.

The love I hold was borne by her;
And now, though far away,
My lonely spirit hears the stir
Of water round the starling spur
Beside the bridge at Grez.

So may that love forever hold
In life an equal pace;
So may that love grow never old,
But, clear and pure and fountain-cold,
Go on from grace to grace.

New Poems

IT'S FORTH ACROSS THE ROARING FOAM

IT'S forth across the roaring foam, and on towards the west,
It's many a lonely league from home, o'er many a mountain crest,
From where the dogs of Scotland call the sheep around the fold,
To where the flags are flying beside the Gates of Gold.

Where all the deep-sea galleons ride that come to bring the corn,
Where falls the fog at eventide and blows the breeze at morn;
It's there that I was sick and sad, alone and poor and cold,
In yon distressful city beside the Gates of Gold.

I slept as one that nothing knows; but far along my way,
Before the morning God rose and planned the coming day;
Afar before me forth he went, as through the sands of old,
And chose the friends to help me beside the Gates of Gold.

I have been near, I have been far, my back's been at the wall,
Yet aye and ever shone the star to guide me through it all:
The love of God, the help of man, they both shall make me bold
Against the gates of darkness as beside the Gates of Gold.

New Poems

AN ENGLISH BREEZE

UP with the sun, the breeze arose,
Across the talking corn she goes,
And smooth she rustles far and wide
Through all the voiceful countryside.

Through all the land her tale she tells;
She spins, she tosses, she compels
The kites, the clouds, the windmill sails
And all the trees in all the dales.

God calls us, and the day prepares
With nimble, gay and gracious airs:
And from Penzance to Maidenhead
The roads last night He watered.

God calls us from inglorious ease,
Forth and to travel with the breeze
While, swift and singing, smooth and strong
She gallops by the fields along.

New Poems

AS IN THEIR FLIGHT THE BIRDS OF SONG

AS in their flight the birds of song
Halt here and there in sweet and sunny dales,
But halt not overlong;
The time one rural song to sing
They pause; then following bounteous gales
Steer forward on the wing:
Sun-servers they, from first to last,
Upon the sun they wait
To ride the sailing blast.

So he awhile in our contested state,
Awhile abode, not longer, for his Sun -
Mother we say, no tenderer name we know -
With whose diviner glow
His early days had shone,
Now to withdraw her radiance had begun.
Or lest a wrong I say, not she withdrew,
But the loud stream of men day after day
And great dust columns of the common way
Between them grew and grew:
And he and she for evermore might yearn,
But to the spring the rivulets not return
Nor to the bosom comes the child again.

And he (O may we fancy so!),
He, feeling time forever flow
And flowing bear him forth and far away
From that dear ingle where his life began
And all his treasure lay -
He, waxing into man,
And ever farther, ever closer wound
In this obstreperous world's ignoble round,
From that poor prospect turned his face away.

THE PIPER

AGAIN I hear you piping, for I know the tune so well, -
You rouse the heart to wander and be free,
Tho' where you learned your music, not the God of song can tell,
For you pipe the open highway and the sea.
O piper, lightly footing, lightly piping on your way,
Tho' your music thrills and pierces far and near,
I tell you you had better pipe to someone else to-day,
For you cannot pipe my fancy from my dear.

You sound the note of travel through the hamlet and the town;
You would lure the holy angels from on high;
And not a man can hear you, but he throws the hammer down
And is off to see the countries ere he die.
But now no more I wander, now unchanging here I stay;
By my love, you find me safely sitting here:
And pipe you ne'er so sweetly, till you pipe the hills away,
You can never pipe my fancy from my dear.

New Poems

TO MRS. MACMARLAND

IN Schnee der Alpen - so it runs
To those divine accords - and here
We dwell in Alpine snows and suns,
A motley crew, for half the year:
A motley crew, we dwell to taste -
A shivering band in hope and fear -
That sun upon the snowy waste,
That Alpine ether cold and clear.

Up from the laboured plains, and up
From low sea-levels, we arise
To drink of that diviner cup
The rarer air, the clearer skies;
For, as the great, old, godly King
From mankind's turbid valley cries,
So all we mountain-lovers sing:
I to the hills will lift mine eyes.

The bells that ring, the peaks that climb,
The frozen snow's unbroken curd
Might yet revindicate in rhyme
The pauseless stream, the absent bird.
In vain - for to the deeps of life
You, lady, you my heart have stirred;
And since you say you love my life,
Be sure I love you for the word.

Of kindness, here I nothing say -
Such loveless kindnesses there are
In that grimacing, common way,
That old, unhonoured social war.
Love but my dog and love my love,
Adore with me a common star -
I value not the rest above
The ashes of a bad cigar.

New Poems

TO MISS CORNISH

THEY tell me, lady, that to-day
On that unknown Australian strand -
Some time ago, so far away -
Another lady joined the band.
She joined the company of those
Lovelily dowered, nobly planned,
Who, smiling, still forgive their foes
And keep their friends in close command.

She, lady, as I learn, was one
Among the many rarely good;
And destined still to be a sun
Through every dark and rainy mood: -
She, as they told me, far had come,
By sea and land, o'er many a rood: -
Admired by all, beloved by some,
She was yourself, I understood.

But, compliment apart and free
From all constraint of verses, may
Goodness and honour, grace and glee,
Attend you ever on your way -
Up to the measure of your will,
Beyond all power of mine to say -
As she and I desire you still,
Miss Cornish, on your natal day.

New Poems

TALES OF ARABIA

YES, friend, I own these tales of Arabia
Smile not, as smiled their flawless originals,
Age-old but yet untamed, for ages
Pass and the magic is undiminished.

Thus, friend, the tales of the old Camaralzaman,
Ayoub, the Slave of Love, or the Calendars,
Blind-eyed and ill-starred royal scions,
Charm us in age as they charmed in childhood.

Fair ones, beyond all numerability,
Beam from the palace, beam on humanity,
Bright-eyed, in truth, yet soul-less houris
Offering pleasure and only pleasure.

Thus they, the venal Muses Arabian,
Unlike, indeed, the nobler divinities,
Greek Gods or old time-honoured muses,
Easily proffer unloved caresses.

Lost, lost, the man who mindeth the minstrelsy;
Since still, in sandy, glittering pleasances,
Cold, stony fruits, gem-like but quite in-
Edible, flatter and wholly starve him.

BEHOLD, AS GOBLINS DARK OF MIEN

BEHOLD, as goblins dark of mien
And portly tyrants dyed with crime
Change, in the transformation scene,
At Christmas, in the pantomime,

Instanter, at the prompter's cough,
The fairy bonnets them, and they
Throw their abhorred carbuncles off
And blossom like the flowers in May.

- So mankind, to angelic eyes,
So, through the scenes of life below,
In life's ironical disguise,
A travesty of man, ye go:

But fear not: ere the curtain fall,
Death in the transformation scene
Steps forward from her pedestal,
Apparent, as the fairy Queen;

And coming, frees you in a trice
From all your lendings - lust of fame,
Ungainly virtue, ugly vice,
Terror and tyranny and shame.

So each, at last himself, for good
In that dear country lays him down,
At last beloved and understood
And pure in feature and renown.

STILL I LOVE TO RHYME

STILL I love to rhyme, and still more, rhyming, to wander
Far from the commoner way;
Old-time trills and falls by the brook-side still do I ponder,
Dreaming to-morrow to-day.

Come here, come, revive me, Sun-God, teach me, Apollo,
Measures descanted before;
Since I ancient verses, I emulous follow,
Prints in the marbles of yore.

Still strange, strange, they sound in old-young raiment invested,
Songs for the brain to forget -
Young song-birds elate to grave old temples benested
Piping and chirruping yet.

Thoughts? No thought has yet unskilled attempted to flutter
Trammelled so vilely in verse;
He who writes but aims at fame and his bread and his butter,
Won with a groan and a curse.

LONG TIME I LAY IN LITTLE EASE

LONG time I lay in little ease
Where, placed by the Turanian,
Marseilles, the many-masted, sees
The blue Mediterranean.

Now songful in the hour of sport,
Now riotous for wages,
She camps around her ancient port,
As ancient of the ages.

Algerian airs through all the place
Unconquerably sally;
Incomparable women pace
The shadows of the alley.

And high o'er dark and graving yard
And where the sky is paler,
The golden virgin of the guard
Shines, beckoning the sailor.

She hears the city roar on high,
Thief, prostitute, and banker;
She sees the masted vessels lie
Immovably at anchor.

She sees the snowy islets dot
The sea's immortal azure,
And If, that castellated spot,
Tower, turret, and embrasure.

FLOWER GOD, GOD OF THE SPRING

FLOWER god, god of the spring, beautiful, bountiful,
Cold-dyed shield in the sky, lover of versicles,
Here I wander in April
Cold, grey-headed; and still to my
Heart, Spring comes with a bound, Spring the deliverer,
Spring, song-leader in woods, chorally resonant;
Spring, flower-planter in meadows,
Child-conductor in willowy
Fields deep dotted with bloom, daisies and crocuses:
Here that child from his heart drinks of eternity:
O child, happy are children!
She still smiles on their innocence,
She, dear mother in God, fostering violets,
Fills earth full of her scents, voices and violins:
Thus one cunning in music
Wakes old chords in the memory:
Thus fair earth in the Spring leads her performances.
One more touch of the bow, smell of the virginal
Green - one more, and my bosom
Feels new life with an ecstasy.

COME, MY BELOVED, HEAR FROM ME

COME, my beloved, hear from me
Tales of the woods or open sea.
Let our aspiring fancy rise
A wren's flight higher toward the skies;
Or far from cities, brown and bare,
Play at the least in open air.
In all the tales men hear us tell
Still let the unfathomed ocean swell,
Or shallower forest sound abroad
Below the lonely stars of God;
In all, let something still be done,
Still in a corner shine the sun,
Slim-ankled maids be fleet of foot,
Nor man disown the rural flute.
Still let the hero from the start
In honest sweat and beats of heart
Push on along the untrodden road
For some inviolate abode.
Still, O beloved, let me hear
The great bell beating far and near-
The odd, unknown, enchanted gong
That on the road hales men along,
That from the mountain calls afar,
That lures a vessel from a star,
And with a still, aerial sound
Makes all the earth enchanted ground.
Love, and the love of life and act
Dance, live and sing through all our furrowed tract;
Till the great God enamoured gives
To him who reads, to him who lives,
That rare and fair romantic strain
That whoso hears must hear again.

SINCE YEARS AGO FOR EVERMORE

SINCE years ago for evermore
My cedar ship I drew to shore;
And to the road and riverbed
And the green, nodding reeds, I said
Mine ignorant and last farewell:
Now with content at home I dwell,
And now divide my sluggish life
Betwixt my verses and my wife:
In vain; for when the lamp is lit
And by the laughing fire I sit,
Still with the tattered atlas spread
Interminable roads I tread.

New Poems

ENVOY FOR "A CHILD'S GARDEN OF VERSES"

WHETHER upon the garden seat
You lounge with your uplifted feet
Under the May's whole Heaven of blue;
Or whether on the sofa you,
No grown up person being by,
Do some soft corner occupy;
Take you this volume in your hands
And enter into other lands,
For lo! (as children feign) suppose
You, hunting in the garden rows,
Or in the lumbered attic, or
The cellar - a nail-studded door
And dark, descending stairway found
That led to kingdoms underground:
There standing, you should hear with ease
Strange birds a-singing, or the trees
Swing in big robber woods, or bells
On many fairy citadels:

There passing through (a step or so -
Neither mamma nor nurse need know!)
From your nice nurseries you would pass,
Like Alice through the Looking-Glass
Or Gerda following Little Ray,
To wondrous countries far away.
Well, and just so this volume can
Transport each little maid or man
Presto from where they live away
Where other children used to play.
As from the house your mother sees
You playing round the garden trees,
So you may see if you but look
Through the windows of this book
Another child far, far away
And in another garden play.
But do not think you can at all,
By knocking on the window, call
That child to hear you. He intent
Is still on his play-business bent.

New Poems

He does not hear, he will not look,
Nor yet be lured out of this book.
For long ago, the truth to say,
He has grown up and gone away;
And it is but a child of air
That lingers in the garden there.

FOR RICHMOND'S GARDEN WALL

WHEN Thomas set this tablet here,
Time laughed at the vain chanticleer;
And ere the moss had dimmed the stone,
Time had defaced that garrison.
Now I in turn keep watch and ward
In my red house, in my walled yard
Of sunflowers, sitting here at ease
With friends and my bright canvases.
But hark, and you may hear quite plain
Time's chuckled laughter in the lane.

New Poems

HAIL, GUEST, AND ENTER FREELY!

HAIL, guest, and enter freely! All you see
Is, for your momentary visit, yours; and we
Who welcome you are but the guests of God,
And know not our departure.

LO, NOW, MY GUEST

LO, now, my guest, if aught amiss were said,
Forgive it and dismiss it from your head.
For me, for you, for all, to close the date,
Pass now the ev'ning sponge across the slate;
And to that spirit of forgiveness keep
Which is the parent and the child of sleep.

SO LIVE, SO LOVE, SO USE THAT FRAGILE HOUR

SO live, so love, so use that fragile hour,
That when the dark hand of the shining power
Shall one from other, wife or husband, take,
The poor survivor may not weep and wake.

AD SE IPSUM

DEAR sir, good-morrow! Five years back,
When you first girded for this arduous track,
And under various whimsical pretexts
Endowed another with your damned defects,
Could you have dreamed in your despondent vein
That the kind God would make your path so plain?
Non nobis, domine! O, may He still
Support my stumbling footsteps on the hill!

BEFORE THIS LITTLE GIFT WAS COME

BEFORE this little gift was come
The little owner had made haste for home;
And from the door of where the eternal dwell,
Looked back on human things and smiled farewell.
O may this grief remain the only one!
O may our house be still a garrison
Of smiling children, and for evermore
The tune of little feet be heard along the floor!

New Poems

GO, LITTLE BOOK - THE ANCIENT PHRASE

GO, little book - the ancient phrase
And still the daintiest - go your ways,
My Otto, over sea and land,
Till you shall come to Nelly's hand.

How shall I your Nelly know?
By her blue eyes and her black brow,
By her fierce and slender look,
And by her goodness, little book!

What shall I say when I come there?
You shall speak her soft and fair:
See - you shall say - the love they send
To greet their unforgotten friend!

Giant Adulpho you shall sing
The next, and then the cradled king:
And the four corners of the roof
Then kindly bless; and to your perch aloof,
Where Balzac all in yellow dressed
And the dear Webster of the west
Encircle the prepotent throne
Of Shakespeare and of Calderon,
Shall climb an upstart.

There with these
You shall give ear to breaking seas
And windmills turning in the breeze,
A distant undetermined din
Without; and you shall hear within
The blazing and the bickering logs,
The crowing child, the yawning dogs,
And ever agile, high and low,
Our Nelly going to and fro.

There shall you all silent sit,
Till, when perchance the lamp is lit
And the day's labour done, she takes
Poor Otto down, and, warming for our sakes,

Perchance beholds, alive and near,
Our distant faces reappear.

MY LOVE WAS WARM

MY love was warm; for that I crossed
The mountains and the sea,
Nor counted that endeavour lost
That gave my love to me.

If that indeed were love at all,
As still, my love, I trow,
By what dear name am I to call
The bond that holds me now

DEDICATORY POEM FOR "UNDERWOODS"

TO her, for I must still regard her
As feminine in her degree,
Who has been my unkind bombarder
Year after year, in grief and glee,
Year after year, with oaken tree;
And yet betweenwhiles my laudator
In terms astonishing to me -
To the Right Reverend The Spectator
I here, a humble dedicator,
Bring the last apples from my tree.

In tones of love, in tones of warning,
She hailed me through my brief career;
And kiss and buffet, night and morning,
Told me my grandmamma was near;
Whether she praised me high and clear
Through her unrivalled circulation,
Or, sanctimonious insincere,
She damned me with a misquotation -
A chequered but a sweet relation,
Say, was it not, my granny dear?

Believe me, granny, altogether
Yours, though perhaps to your surprise.
Oft have you spruced my wounded feather,
Oft brought a light into my eyes -
For notice still the writer cries.
In any civil age or nation,
The book that is not talked of dies.
So that shall be my termination:
Whether in praise or execration,
Still, if you love me, criticise!

FAREWELL

FAREWELL, and when forth
I through the Golden Gates to Golden Isles
Steer without smiling, through the sea of smiles,
Isle upon isle, in the seas of the south,
Isle upon island, sea upon sea,
Why should I sail, why should the breeze?
I have been young, and I have counted friends.
A hopeless sail I spread, too late, too late.
Why should I from isle to isle
Sail, a hopeless sailor?

New Poems

THE FAR-FARERS

THE broad sun,
The bright day:
White sails
On the blue bay:
The far-farers
Draw away.

Light the fires
And close the door.
To the old homes,
To the loved shore,
The far-farers
Return no more.

New Poems

HOME, MY LITTLE CHILDREN, HERE ARE SONGS FOR YOU

COME, my little children, here are songs for you;
Some are short and some are long, and all, all are new.
You must learn to sing them very small and clear,
Very true to time and tune and pleasing to the ear.

Mark the note that rises, mark the notes that fall,
Mark the time when broken, and the swing of it all.
So when night is come, and you have gone to bed,
All the songs you love to sing shall echo in your head.

COME FROM THE DAISIED MEADOWS

HOME from the daisied meadows, where you linger yet -
Home, golden-headed playmate, ere the sun is set;
For the dews are falling fast
And the night has come at last.
Home with you, home and lay your little head at rest,
Safe, safe, my little darling, on your mother's breast.
Lullaby, darling; your mother is watching you;
she'll be your guardian and shield.
Lullaby, slumber, my darling, till morning be
bright upon mountain and field.
Long, long the shadows fall.
All white and smooth at home your little bed is laid.
All round your head be angels.

New Poems

EARLY IN THE MORNING I HEAR ON YOUR PIANO

EARLY in the morning I hear on your piano
You (at least, I guess it's you) proceed to learn to play.
Mostly little minds should take and tackle their piano
While the birds are singing in the morning of the day.

New Poems

FAIR ISLE AT SEA

FAIR Isle at Sea - thy lovely name
Soft in my ear like music came.
That sea I loved, and once or twice
I touched at isles of Paradise.

LOUD AND LOW IN THE CHIMNEY

LOUD and low in the chimney
The squalls suspire;
Then like an answer dwindles
And glows the fire,
And the chamber reddens and darkens
In time like taken breath.
Near by the sounding chimney
The youth apart
Hearkens with changing colour
And leaping heart,
And hears in the coil of the tempest
The voice of love and death.
Love on high in the flute-like
And tender notes
Sounds as from April meadows
And hillside cotes;
But the deep wood wind in the chimney
Utters the slogan of death.

New Poems

I LOVE TO BE WARM BY THE RED FIRESIDE

I LOVE to be warm by the red fireside,
I love to be wet with rain:
I love to be welcome at lamplit doors,
And leave the doors again.

New Poems

AT LAST SHE COMES

AT last she comes, O never more
In this dear patience of my pain
To leave me lonely as before,
Or leave my soul alone again.

MINE EYES WERE SWIFT TO KNOW THEE

MINE eyes were swift to know thee, and my heart
As swift to love. I did become at once
Thine wholly, thine unalterably, thine
In honourable service, pure intent,
Steadfast excess of love and laughing care:
And as she was, so am, and so shall be.
I knew thee helpful, knew thee true, knew thee
And Pity bedfellows: I heard thy talk
With answerable throbbings. On the stream,
Deep, swift, and clear, the lilies floated; fish
Through the shadows ran. There, thou and I
Read Kindness in our eyes and closed the match.

FIXED IS THE DOOM

FIXED is the doom; and to the last of years
Teacher and taught, friend, lover, parent, child,
Each walks, though near, yet separate; each beholds
His dear ones shine beyond him like the stars.
We also, love, forever dwell apart;
With cries approach, with cries behold the gulph,
The Unvaulted; as two great eagles that do wheel in air
Above a mountain, and with screams confer,
Far heard athwart the cedars.
Yet the years
Shall bring us ever nearer; day by day
Endearing, week by week, till death at last
Dissolve that long divorce. By faith we love,
Not knowledge; and by faith, though far removed,
Dwell as in perfect nearness, heart to heart.
We but excuse
Those things we merely are; and to our souls
A brave deception cherish.
So from unhappy war a man returns
Unfearing, or the seaman from the deep;
So from cool night and woodlands to a feast
May someone enter, and still breathe of dews,
And in her eyes still wear the dusky night.

MEN ARE HEAVEN'S PIERS

MEN are Heaven's piers; they evermore
Unwearying bear the skyey floor;
Man's theatre they bear with ease,
Unfrowning cariatides!
I, for my wife, the sun uphold,
Or, dozing, strike the seasons cold.
She, on her side, in fairy-wise
Deals in diviner mysteries,
By spells to make the fuel burn
And keep the parlour warm, to turn
Water to wine, and stones to bread,
By her unconquered hero-head.
A naked Adam, naked Eve,
Alone the primal bower we weave;
Sequestered in the seas of life,
A Crusoe couple, man and wife,
With all our good, with all our will,
Our unfrequented isle we fill;
And victor in day's petty wars,
Each for the other lights the stars.
Come then, my Eve, and to and fro
Let us about our garden go;
And, grateful-hearted, hand in hand
Revisit all our tillage land,
And marvel at our strange estate,
For hooded ruin at the gate
Sits watchful, and the angels fear
To see us tread so boldly here.
Meanwhile, my Eve, with flower and grass
Our perishable days we pass;
Far more the thorn observe - and see
How our enormous sins go free -
Nor less admire, beside the rose,
How far a little virtue goes.

THE ANGLER ROSE, HE TOOK HIS ROD

THE angler rose, he took his rod,
He kneeled and made his prayers to God.
The living God sat overhead:
The angler tripped, the eels were fed

New Poems

SPRING CAROL

WHEN loud by landside streamlets gush,
And clear in the greenwood quires the thrush,
With sun on the meadows
And songs in the shadows
Comes again to me
The gift of the tongues of the lea,
The gift of the tongues of meadows.

Straightway my olden heart returns
And dances with the dancing burns;
It sings with the sparrows;
To the rain and the (grimy) barrows
Sings my heart aloud -
To the silver-bellied cloud,
To the silver rainy arrows.

It bears the song of the skylark down,
And it hears the singing of the town;
And youth on the highways
And lovers in byways
Follows and sees:
And hearkens the song of the leas
And sings the songs of the highways.

So when the earth is alive with gods,
And the lusty ploughman breaks the sod,
And the grass sings in the meadows,
And the flowers smile in the shadows,
Sits my heart at ease,
Hearing the song of the leas,
Singing the songs of the meadows.

TO WHAT SHALL I COMPARE HER?

TO what shall I compare her,
That is as fair as she?
For she is fairer - fairer
Than the sea.
What shall be likened to her,
The sainted of my youth?
For she is truer - truer
Than the truth.

As the stars are from the sleeper,
Her heart is hid from me;
For she is deeper - deeper
Than the sea.
Yet in my dreams I view her
Flush rosy with new ruth -
Dreams! Ah, may these prove truer
Than the truth.

WHEN THE SUN COMES AFTER RAIN

WHEN the sun comes after rain
And the bird is in the blue,
The girls go down the lane
Two by two.

When the sun comes after shadow
And the singing of the showers,
The girls go up the meadow,
Fair as flowers.

When the eve comes dusky red
And the moon succeeds the sun,
The girls go home to bed
One by one.

And when life draws to its even
And the day of man is past,
They shall all go home to heaven,
Home at last.

LATE, O MILLER

LATE, O miller,
The birds are silent,
The darkness falls.
In the house the lights are lighted.
See, in the valley they twinkle,
The lights of home.
Late, O lovers,
The night is at hand;
Silence and darkness
Clothe the land.

New Poems

TO FRIENDS AT HOME

TO friends at home, the lone, the admired, the lost
The gracious old, the lovely young, to May
The fair, December the beloved,
These from my blue horizon and green isles,
These from this pinnacle of distances I,
The unforgetful, dedicate.

I, WHOM APOLLO SOMETIME VISITED

I, WHOM Apollo sometime visited,
Or feigned to visit, now, my day being done,
Do slumber wholly; nor shall know at all
The weariness of changes; nor perceive
Immeasurable sands of centuries
Drink of the blanching ink, or the loud sound
Of generations beat the music down.

New Poems

TEMPEST TOSSED AND SORE AFFLICTED

TEMPEST tossed and sore afflicted, sin defiled and care oppressed,
Come to me, all ye that labour; come, and I will give ye rest.
Fear no more, O doubting hearted; weep no more, O weeping eye!
Lo, the voice of your redeemer; lo, the songful morning near.

Here one hour you toil and combat, sin and suffer, bleed and die;
In my father's quiet mansion soon to lay your burden by.
Bear a moment, heavy laden, weary hand and weeping eye.
Lo, the feet of your deliverer; lo, the hour of freedom here.

VARIANT FORM OF THE PRECEDING POEM

COME to me, all ye that labour; I will give your spirits rest;
Here apart in starry quiet I will give you rest.
Come to me, ye heavy laden, sin defiled and care opprest,
In your father's quiet mansions, soon to prove a welcome guest.
But an hour you bear your trial, sin and suffer, bleed and die;
But an hour you toil and combat here in day's inspiring eye.
See the feet of your deliverer; lo, the hour of freedom nigh.

New Poems

I NOW, O FRIEND, WHOM NOISELESSLY THE SNOWS

I NOW, O friend, whom noiselessly the snows
Settle around, and whose small chamber grows
Dusk as the sloping window takes its load:

* * * * *

The kindly hill, as to complete our hap,
Has ta'en us in the shelter of her lap;
Well sheltered in our slender grove of trees
And ring of walls, we sit between her knees;
A disused quarry, paved with rose plots, hung
With clematis, the barren womb whence sprung
The crow-stepped house itself, that now far seen
Stands, like a bather, to the neck in green.
A disused quarry, furnished with a seat
Sacred to pipes and meditation meet
For such a sunny and retired nook.
There in the clear, warm mornings many a book
Has vied with the fair prospect of the hills
That, vale on vale, rough brae on brae, upfills
Halfway to the zenith all the vacant sky
To keep my loose attention. . . .
Horace has sat with me whole mornings through:
And Montaigne gossiped, fairly false and true;
And chattering Pepys, and a few beside
That suit the easy vein, the quiet tide,
The calm and certain stay of garden-life,
Far sunk from all the thunderous roar of strife.
There is about the small secluded place
A garnish of old times; a certain grace
Of pensive memories lays about the braes:
The old chestnuts gossip tales of bygone days.
Here, where some wandering preacher, blest Lazil,
Perhaps, or Peden, on the middle hill
Had made his secret church, in rain or snow,
He cheers the chosen residue from woe.
All night the doors stood open, come who might,
The hounded kebbock mat the mud all night.

Nor are there wanting later tales; of how
Prince Charlie's Highlanders . . .

* * * * *

I have had talents, too. In life's first hour
God crowned with benefits my childish head.
Flower after flower, I plucked them; flower by flower
Cast them behind me, ruined, withered, dead.
Full many a shining godhead disappeared.
From the bright rank that once adorned her brow
The old child's Olympus

* * * * *

Gone are the fair old dreams, and one by one,
As, one by one, the means to reach them went,
As, one by one, the stars in riot and disgrace,
I squandered what . . .

There shut the door, alas! on many a hope
Too many;
My face is set to the autumnal slope,
Where the loud winds shall . . .

There shut the door, alas! on many a hope,
And yet some hopes remain that shall decide
My rest of years and down the autumnal slope.

* * * * *

Gone are the quiet twilight dreams that I
Loved, as all men have loved them; gone!
I have great dreams, and still they stir my soul on high -
Dreams of the knight's stout heart and tempered will.
Not in Elysian lands they take their way;
Not as of yore across the gay champaign,
Towards some dream city, towered . . .
and my . . .
The path winds forth before me, sweet and plain,
Not now; but though beneath a stone-grey sky
November's russet woodlands toss and wail,

New Poems

Still the white road goes thro' them, still may I,
Strong in new purpose, God, may still prevail.

* * * * *

I and my like, improvident sailors!

* * * * *

At whose light fall awaking, all my heart
Grew populous with gracious, favoured thought,
And all night long thereafter, hour by hour,
The pageant of dead love before my eyes
Went proudly, and old hopes with downcast head
Followed like Kings, subdued in Rome's imperial hour,
Followed the car; and I . . .

New Poems

SINCE THOU HAST GIVEN ME THIS GOOD HOPE, O GOD

SINCE thou hast given me this good hope, O God,
That while my footsteps tread the flowery sod
And the great woods embower me, and white dawn
And purple even sweetly lead me on
From day to day, and night to night, O God,
My life shall no wise miss the light of love;
But ever climbing, climb above
Man's one poor star, man's supine lands,
Into the azure steadfastness of death,
My life shall no wise lack the light of love,
My hands not lack the loving touch of hands;
But day by day, while yet I draw my breath,
And day by day, unto my last of years,
I shall be one that has a perfect friend.
Her heart shall taste my laughter and my tears,
And her kind eyes shall lead me to the end.

New Poems

GOD GAVE TO ME A CHILD IN PART

GOD gave to me a child in part,
Yet wholly gave the father's heart:
Child of my soul, O whither now,
Unborn, unmothered, goest thou?

You came, you went, and no man wist;
Hapless, my child, no breast you kist;
On no dear knees, a privileged babbler, clomb,
Nor knew the kindly feel of home.

My voice may reach you, O my dear-
A father's voice perhaps the child may hear;
And, pitying, you may turn your view
On that poor father whom you never knew.

Alas! alone he sits, who then,
Immortal among mortal men,
Sat hand in hand with love, and all day through
With your dear mother wondered over you.

OVER THE LAND IS APRIL

OVER the land is April,
Over my heart a rose;
Over the high, brown mountain
The sound of singing goes.
Say, love, do you hear me,
Hear my sonnets ring?
Over the high, brown mountain,
Love, do you hear me sing?

By highway, love, and byway
The snows succeed the rose.
Over the high, brown mountain
The wind of winter blows.
Say, love, do you hear me,
Hear my sonnets ring?
Over the high, brown mountain
I sound the song of spring,
I throw the flowers of spring.
Do you hear the song of spring?
Hear you the songs of spring?

New Poems

LIGHT AS THE LINNET ON MY WAY I START

LIGHT as the linnet on my way I start,
For all my pack I bear a chartered heart.
Forth on the world without a guide or chart,
Content to know, through all man's varying fates,
The eternal woman by the wayside waits.

COME, HERE IS ADIEU TO THE CITY

COME, here is adieu to the city
And hurrah for the country again.
The broad road lies before me
Watered with last night's rain.
The timbered country woos me
With many a high and bough;
And again in the shining fallows
The ploughman follows the plough.

The whole year's sweat and study,
And the whole year's sowing time,
Comes now to the perfect harvest,
And ripens now into rhyme.
For we that sow in the Autumn,
We reap our grain in the Spring,
And we that go sowing and weeping
Return to reap and sing.

New Poems

IT BLOWS A SNOWING GALE

IT blows a snowing gale in the winter of the year;
The boats are on the sea and the crews are on the pier.
The needle of the vane, it is veering to and fro,
A flash of sun is on the veering of the vane.
Autumn leaves and rain,
The passion of the gale.

NE SIT ANCILLAE TIBI AMOR PUDOR

THERE'S just a twinkle in your eye
That seems to say I MIGHT, if I
Were only bold enough to try
An arm about your waist.
I hear, too, as you come and go,
That pretty nervous laugh, you know;
And then your cap is always so
Coquettishly displaced.

Your cap! the word's profanely said.
That little top-knot, white and red,
That quaintly crowns your graceful head,
No bigger than a flower,
Is set with such a witching art,
Is so provocatively smart,
I'd like to wear it on my heart,
An order for an hour!

O graceful housemaid, tall and fair,
I love your shy imperial air,
And always loiter on the stair
When you are going by.
A strict reserve the fates demand;
But, when to let you pass I stand,
Sometimes by chance I touch your hand
And sometimes catch your eye.

New Poems

TO ALL THAT LOVE THE FAR AND BLUE

TO all that love the far and blue:
Whether, from dawn to eve, on foot
The fleeing corners ye pursue,
Nor weary of the vain pursuit;
Or whether down the singing stream,
Paddle in hand, jocund ye shoot,
To splash beside the splashing bream
Or anchor by the willow root:

Or, bolder, from the narrow shore
Put forth, that cedar ark to steer,
Among the seabirds and the roar
Of the great sea, profound and clear;
Or, lastly if in heart ye roam,
Not caring to do else, and hear,
Safe sitting by the fire at home,
Footfalls in Utah or Pamere:

Though long the way, though hard to bear
The sun and rain, the dust and dew;
Though still attainment and despair
Inter the old, despoil the new;
There shall at length, be sure, O friends,
Howe'er ye steer, whate'er ye do -
At length, and at the end of ends,
The golden city come in view.

THOU STRAINEST THROUGH THE MOUNTAIN FERN
(A FRAGMENT)

THOU strainest through the mountain fern,
A most exiguously thin Burn.
For all thy foam, for all thy din,
Thee shall the pallid lake inurn,
With well-a-day for Mr. Swin-Burne!
Take then this quarto in thy fin
And, O thou stoker huge and stern,
The whole affair, outside and in,
Burn!
But save the true poetic kin,
The works of Mr. Robert Burn'
And William Wordsworth upon Tin-Tern!

New Poems

TO ROSABELLE

WHEN my young lady has grown great and staid,
And in long raiment wondrously arrayed,
She may take pleasure with a smile to know
How she delighted men-folk long ago.
For her long after, then, this tale I tell
Of the two fans and fairy Rosabelle.
Hot was the day; her weary sire and I
Sat in our chairs companionably nigh,
Each with a headache sat her sire and I.

Instant the hostess waked: she viewed the scene,
Divined the giants' languor by their mien,
And with hospitable care
Tackled at once an Atlantean chair.
Her pigmy stature scarce attained the seat -
She dragged it where she would, and with her feet
Surmounted; thence, a Phaeton launched, she crowned
The vast plateau of the piano, found
And culled a pair of fans; wherewith equipped,
Our mountaineer back to the level slipped;
And being landed, with considerate eyes,
Betwixt her elders dealt her double prize;
The small to me, the greater to her sire.
As painters now advance and now retire
Before the growing canvas, and anon
Once more approach and put the climax on:
So she awhile withdrew, her piece she viewed -
For half a moment half supposed it good -
Spied her mistake, nor sooner spied than ran
To remedy; and with the greater fan,
In gracious better thought, equipped the guest.

From ill to well, from better on to best,
Arts move; the homely, like the plastic kind;
And high ideals fired that infant mind.
Once more she backed, once more a space apart
Considered and reviewed her work of art:
Doubtful at first, and gravely yet awhile;
Till all her features blossomed in a smile.

And the child, waking at the call of bliss,
To each she ran, and took and gave a kiss.

NOW BARE TO THE BEHOLDER'S EYE

NOW bare to the beholder's eye
Your late denuded bindings lie,
Subsiding slowly where they fell,
A disinvested citadel;
The obdurate corset, Cupid's foe,
The Dutchman's breeches frilled below.
Those that the lover notes to note,
And white and crackling petticoat.

From these, that on the ground repose,
Their lady lately re-arose;
And laying by the lady's name,
A living woman re-became.
Of her, that from the public eye
They do enclose and fortify,
Now, lying scattered as they fell,
An indiscreeter tale they tell:
Of that more soft and secret her
Whose daylong fortresses they were,
By fading warmth, by lingering print,
These now discarded scabbards hint.

A twofold change the ladies know:
First, in the morn the bugles blow,
And they, with floral hues and scents,
Man their beribboned battlements.
But let the stars appear, and they
Shed inhumanities away;
And from the changeling fashion see,
Through comic and through sweet degree,
In nature's toilet unsurpassed,
Forth leaps the laughing girl at last.

New Poems

THE BOUR-TREE DEN

CLINKUM-CLANK in the rain they ride,
Down by the braes and the grey sea-side;
Clinkum-clank by stane and cairn,
Weary fa' their horse-shoe-airn!

Loud on the causey, saft on the sand,
Round they rade by the tail of the land;
Round and up by the Bour-Tree Den,
Weary fa' the red-coat men!

Aft hae I gane where they hae rade
And straigled in the gowden brooms -
Aft hae I gane, a saikless maid,
And O! sae bonny as the bour-tree blooms!

Wi' swords and guns they wanton there,
Wi' red, red coats and braw, braw plumes.
But I gaed wi' my gowden hair,
And O! sae bonny as the bour-tree blooms!

I ran, a little hempie lass,
In the sand and the bent grass,
Or took and kilted my small coats
To play in the beached fisher-boats.

I waded deep and I ran fast,
I was as lean as a lugger's mast,
I was as brown as a fisher's creel,
And I liked my life unco weel.

They blew a trumpet at the cross,
Some forty men, both foot and horse.
A'body cam to hear and see,
And wha, among the rest, but me.
My lips were saut wi' the saut air,
My face was brown, my feet were bare
The wind had ravelled my tautit hair,
And I thought shame to be standing there.

New Poems

Ae man there in the thick of the throng
Sat in his saddle, straight and strong.
I looked at him and he at me,
And he was a master-man to see.
. .. And who is this yin? and who is yon
That has the bonny lendings on?
That sits and looks sae braw and crouse?
. .. Mister Frank o' the Big House!

I gaed my lane beside the sea;
The wind it blew in bush and tree,
The wind blew in bush and bent:
Muckle I saw, and muckle kent!

Between the beach and the sea-hill
I sat my lane and grat my fill -
I was sae clarty and hard and dark,
And like the kye in the cow park!

There fell a battle far in the north;
The evil news gaed back and forth,
And back and forth by brae and bent
Hider and hunter cam and went:
The hunter clattered horse-shoe-airn
By causey-crest and hill-top cairn;
The hider, in by shag and shench,
Crept on his wame and little lench.

The eastland wind blew shrill and snell,
The stars arose, the gloaming fell,
The firelight shone in window and door
When Mr. Frank cam here to shore.
He hirpled up by the links and the lane,
And chappit laigh in the back-door-stane.
My faither gaed, and up wi' his han'!
. .. Is this Mr. Frank, or a beggarman?

I have mistrysted sair, he said,
But let me into fire and bed;
Let me in, for auld lang syne,
And give me a dram of the brandy wine.

They hid him in the Bour-Tree Den,

And I thought it strange to gang my lane;
I thought it strange, I thought it sweet,
To gang there on my naked feet.
In the mirk night, when the boats were at sea,
I passed the burn abune the knee;
In the mirk night, when the folks were asleep,
I had a tryst in the den to keep.

Late and air', when the folks were asleep,
I had a tryst, a tryst to keep,
I had a lad that lippened to me,
And bour-tree blossom is fair to see!

O' the bour-tree leaves I busked his bed,
The mune was siller, the dawn was red:
Was nae man there but him and me -
And bour-tree blossom is fair to see!

Unco weather hae we been through:
The mune glowered, and the wind blew,
And the rain it rained on him and me,
And bour-tree blossom is fair to see!

Dwelling his lane but house or hauld,
Aft he was wet and aft was cauld;
I warmed him wi' my briest and knee -
And bour-tree blossom is fair to see!

There was nae voice of beast ae man,
But the tree soughed and the burn ran,
And we heard the ae voice of the sea:
Bour-tree blossom is fair to see!

New Poems

SONNETS

I.

NOR judge me light, tho' light at times I seem,
And lightly in the stress of fortune bear
The innumerable flaws of changeful care -
Nor judge me light for this, nor rashly deem
(Office forbid to mortals, kept supreme
And separate the prerogative of God!)
That seaman idle who is borne abroad
To the far haven by the favouring stream.
Not he alone that to contrarious seas
Opposes, all night long, the unwearied oar,
Not he alone, by high success endeared,
Shall reach the Port; but, winged, with some light breeze
Shall they, with upright keels, pass in before
Whom easy Taste, the golden pilot, steered.

II.

So shall this book wax like unto a well,
Fairy with mirrored flowers about the brim,
Or like some tarn that wailing curlews skim,
Glassing the sallow uplands or brown fell;
And so, as men go down into a dell
(Weary with noon) to find relief and shade,
When on the uneasy sick-bed we are laid,
We shall go down into thy book, and tell
The leaves, once blank, to build again for us
Old summer dead and ruined, and the time
Of later autumn with the corn in stook.
So shalt thou stint the meagre winter thus
Of his projected triumph, and the rime
Shall melt before the sunshine in thy book.

III.

I have a hoard of treasure in my breast;
The grange of memory steams against the door,
Full of my bygone lifetime's garnered store -
Old pleasures crowned with sorrow for a zest,

Old sorrow grown a joy, old penance blest,
Chastened remembrance of the sins of yore
That, like a new evangel, more and more
Supports our halting will toward the best.
Ah! what to us the barren after years
May bring of joy or sorrow, who can tell?
O, knowing not, who cares? It may be well
That we shall find old pleasures and old fears,
And our remembered childhood seen thro' tears,
The best of Heaven and the worst of Hell.

IV.

As starts the absent dreamer when a train,
Suddenly disengulphed below his feet,
Roars forth into the sunlight, to its seat
My soul was shaken with immediate pain
Intolerable as the scanty breath
Of that one word blew utterly away
The fragile mist of fair deceit that lay
O'er the bleak years that severed me from death.
Yes, at the sight I quailed; but, not unwise
Or not, O God, without some nervous thread
Of that best valour, Patience, bowed my head,
And with firm bosom and most steadfast eyes,
Strong in all high resolve, prepared to tread
The unlovely path that leads me toward the skies.

V.

Not undelightful, friend, our rustic ease
To grateful hearts; for by especial hap,
Deep nested in the hill's enormous lap,
With its own ring of walls and grove of trees,
Sits, in deep shelter, our small cottage - nor
Far-off is seen, rose carpeted and hung
With clematis, the quarry whence she sprung,
O mater pulchra filia pulchrior,
Whither in early spring, unharnessed folk,
We join the pairing swallows, glad to stay
Where, loosened in the hills, remote, unseen,
From its tall trees, it breathes a slender smoke
To heaven, and in the noon of sultry day
Stands, coolly buried, to the neck in green.

VI.

As in the hostel by the bridge I sate,
Nailed with indifference fondly deemed complete,
And (O strange chance, more sorrowful than sweet)
The counterfeit of her that was my fate,
Dressed in like vesture, graceful and sedate,
Went quietly up the vacant village street,
The still small sound of her most dainty feet
Shook, like a trumpet blast, my soul's estate.
Instant revolt ran riot through my brain,
And all night long, thereafter, hour by hour,
The pageant of dead love before my eyes
Went proudly; and old hopes, broke loose again
From the restraint of wisely temperate power,
With ineffectual ardour sought to rise.

VII.

The strong man's hand, the snow-cool head of age,
The certain-footed sympathies of youth -
These, and that lofty passion after truth,
Hunger unsatisfied in priest or sage
Or the great men of former years, he needs
That not unworthily would dare to sing
(Hard task!) black care's inevitable ring
Settling with years upon the heart that feeds
Incessantly on glory. Year by year
The narrowing toil grows closer round his feet;
With disenchanting touch rude-handed time
The unlovely web discloses, and strange fear
Leads him at last to eld's inclement seat,
The bitter north of life - a frozen clime.

VIII.

As Daniel, bird-alone, in that far land,
Kneeling in fervent prayer, with heart-sick eyes
Turned thro' the casement toward the westering skies;
Or as untamed Elijah, that red brand
Among the starry prophets; or that band
And company of Faithful sanctities
Who in all times, when persecutions rise,

Cherish forgotten creeds with fostering hand:
Such do ye seem to me, light-hearted crew,
O turned to friendly arts with all your will,
That keep a little chapel sacred still,
One rood of Holy-land in this bleak earth
Sequestered still (our homage surely due!)
To the twin Gods of mirthful wine and mirth.

About my fields, in the broad sun
And blaze of noon, there goeth one,
Barefoot and robed in blue, to scan
With the hard eye of the husbandman
My harvests and my cattle. Her,
When even puts the birds astir
And day has set in the great woods,
We seek, among her garden roods,
With bells and cries in vain: the while
Lamps, plate, and the decanter smile
On the forgotten board. But she,
Deaf, blind, and prone on face and knee,
Forgets time, family, and feast,
And digs like a demented beast.

Tall as a guardsman, pale as the east at dawn,
Who strides in strange apparel on the lawn?
Rails for his breakfast? routs his vassals out
(Like boys escaped from school) with song and shout?
Kind and unkind, his Maker's final freak,
Part we deride the child, part dread the antique!
See where his gang, like frogs, among the dew
Crouch at their duty, an unquiet crew;
Adjust their staring kilts; and their swift eyes
Turn still to him who sits to supervise.
He in the midst, perched on a fallen tree,
Eyes them at labour; and, guitar on knee,
Now ministers alarm, now scatters joy,
Now twangs a halting chord, now tweaks a boy.
Thorough in all, my resolute vizier
Plays both the despot and the volunteer,
Exacts with fines obedience to my laws,
And for his music, too, exacts applause.
The Adorner of the uncomely - those
Amidst whose tall battalions goes

Her pretty person out and in
All day with an endearing din,
Of censure and encouragement;
And when all else is tried in vain
See her sit down and weep again.
She weeps to conquer;
She varies on her grenadiers
From satire up to girlish tears!

Or rather to behold her when
She plies for me the unresting pen,
And when the loud assault of squalls
Resounds upon the roof and walls,
And the low thunder growls and I
Raise my dictating voice on high.

What glory for a boy of ten
Who now must three gigantic men
And two enormous, dapple grey
New Zealand pack-horses array
And lead, and wisely resolute
Our day-long business execute
In the far shore-side town. His soul
Glows in his bosom like a coal;
His innocent eyes glitter again,
And his hand trembles on the rein.
Once he reviews his whole command,
And chivalrously planting hand
On hip - a borrowed attitude -
Rides off downhill into the wood.

I meanwhile in the populous house apart
Sit snugly chambered, and my silent art
Uninterrupted, unremitting ply
Before the dawn, by morning lamplight, by
The glow of smelting noon, and when the sun
Dips past my westering hill and day is done;
So, bending still over my trade of words,
I hear the morning and the evening birds,
The morning and the evening stars behold;
So there apart I sit as once of old
Napier in wizard Merchiston; and my
Brown innocent aides in home and husbandry

New Poems

Wonder askance. What ails the boss? they ask.
Him, richest of the rich, an endless task
Before the earliest birds or servants stir
Calls and detains him daylong prisoner?
He whose innumerable dollars hewed
This cleft in the boar and devil-haunted wood,
And bade therein, from sun to seas and skies,
His many-windowed, painted palace rise
Red-roofed, blue-walled, a rainbow on the hill,
A wonder in the forest glade: he still,

Unthinkable Aladdin, dawn and dark,
Scribbles and scribbles, like a German clerk.
We see the fact, but tell, O tell us why?
My reverend washman and wise butler cry.
Meanwhile at times the manifold
Imperishable perfumes of the past
And coloured pictures rise on me thick and fast:
And I remember the white rime, the loud
Lamplitten city, shops, and the changing crowd;
And I remember home and the old time,
The winding river, the white moving rhyme,
The autumn robin by the river-side
That pipes in the grey eve.

The old lady (so they say), but I
Admire your young vitality.
Still brisk of foot, still busy and keen
In and about and up and down.

I hear you pass with bustling feet
The long verandahs round, and beat
Your bell, and "Lotu! Lotu! " cry;
Thus calling our queer company,
In morning or in evening dim,
To prayers and the oft mangled hymn.

All day you watch across the sky
The silent, shining cloudlands ply,
That, huge as countries, swift as birds,
Beshade the isles by halves and thirds,
Till each with battlemented crest
Stands anchored in the ensanguined west,

An Alp enchanted. All the day
You hear the exuberant wind at play,
In vast, unbroken voice uplift,
In roaring tree, round whistling clift.

New Poems

AIR OF DIABELLI'S

CALL it to mind, O my love.
Dear were your eyes as the day,
Bright as the day and the sky;
Like the stream of gold and the sky above,
Dear were your eyes in the grey.
We have lived, my love, O, we have lived, my love!
Now along the silent river, azure
Through the sky's inverted image,
Softly swam the boat that bore our love,
Swiftly ran the shallow of our love
Through the heaven's inverted image,
In the reedy mazes round the river.
See along the silent river,

See of old the lover's shallop steer.
Berried brake and reedy island,
Heaven below and only heaven above.
Through the sky's inverted image
Swiftly swam the boat that bore our love.
Berried brake and reedy island,
Mirrored flower and shallop gliding by.
All the earth and all the sky were ours,
Silent sat the wafted lovers,
Bound with grain and watched by all the sky,
Hand to hand and eye to ... eye.

Days of April, airs of Eden,
Call to mind how bright the vanished angel hours,
Golden hours of evening,
When our boat drew homeward filled with flowers.
O darling, call them to mind; love the past, my love.
Days of April, airs of Eden.
How the glory died through golden hours,
And the shining moon arising;
How the boat drew homeward filled with flowers.
Age and winter close us slowly in.

Level river, cloudless heaven,
Islanded reed mazes, silver weirs;

New Poems

How the silent boat with silver
Threads the inverted forest as she goes,
Broke the trembling green of mirrored trees.
O, remember, and remember
How the berries hung in garlands.

Still in the river see the shallop floats.
Hark! Chimes the falling oar.
Still in the mind
Hark to the song of the past!
Dream, and they pass in their dreams.

Those that loved of yore, O those that loved of yore!
Hark through the stillness, O darling, hark!
Through it all the ear of the mind

Knows the boat of love. Hark!
Chimes the falling oar.

O half in vain they grew old.

Now the halcyon days are over,
Age and winter close us slowly round,
And these sounds at fall of even
Dim the sight and muffle all the sound.
And at the married fireside, sleep of soul and sleep of fancy,
Joan and Darby.
Silence of the world without a sound;
And beside the winter faggot

Joan and Darby sit and dose and dream and wake -
Dream they hear the flowing, singing river,
See the berries in the island brake;
Dream they hear the weir,
See the gliding shallop mar the stream.
Hark! in your dreams do you hear?

Snow has filled the drifted forest;
Ice has bound the . ... stream.
Frost has bound our flowing river;
Snow has whitened all our island brake.

Berried brake and reedy island,

Heaven below and only heaven above azure
Through the sky's inverted image
Safely swam the boat that bore our love.
Dear were your eyes as the day,
Bright ran the stream, bright hung the sky above.
Days of April, airs of Eden.
How the glory died through golden hours,
And the shining moon arising,
How the boat drew homeward filled with flowers.
Bright were your eyes in the night:
We have lived, my love;
O, we have loved, my love.
Now the . .. days are over,
Age and winter close us slowly round.

Vainly time departs, and vainly
Age and winter come and close us round.

Hark the river's long continuous sound.

Hear the river ripples in the reeds.

Lo, in dreams they see their shallop
Run the lilies down and drown the weeds
Mid the sound of crackling faggots.
So in dreams the new created
Happy past returns, to-day recedes,
And they hear once more,

From the old years,
Yesterday returns, to-day recedes,
And they hear with aged hearing warbles

Love's own river ripple in the weeds.
And again the lover's shallop;
Lo, the shallop sheds the streaming weeds;
And afar in foreign countries
In the ears of aged lovers.

And again in winter evens
Starred with lilies . ... with stirring weeds.
In these ears of aged lovers
Love's own river ripples in the reeds.

New Poems

EPITAPHIUM EROTII

HERE lies Erotion, whom at six years old
Fate pilfered. Stranger (when I too am cold,
Who shall succeed me in my rural field),
To this small spirit annual honours yield!
Bright be thy hearth, hale be thy babes, I crave
And this, in thy green farm, the only grave.

DE M. ANTONIO

NOW Antoninus, in a smiling age,
Counts of his life the fifteenth finished stage.
The rounded days and the safe years he sees,
Nor fears death's water mounting round his knees.
To him remembering not one day is sad,
Not one but that its memory makes him glad.
So good men lengthen life; and to recall
The past is to have twice enjoyed it all.

New Poems

AD MAGISTRUM LUDI
(UNFINISHED DRAFT.)

NOW in the sky
And on the hearth of
Now in a drawer the direful cane,
That sceptre of the . ... reign,
And the long hawser, that on the back
Of Marsyas fell with many a whack,
Twice hardened out of Scythian hides,
Now sleep till the October ides.

In summer if the boys be well.

New Poems

AD NEPOTEM

O NEPOS, twice my neigh(b)our (since at home
We're door by door, by Flora's temple dome;
And in the country, still conjoined by fate,
Behold our villas standing gate by gate),
Thou hast a daughter, dearer far than life -
Thy image and the image of thy wife.
Thy image and thy wife's, and be it so!

But why for her, { neglect the flowing } can
{ O Nepos, leave the }

And lose the prime of thy Falernian?
Hoard casks of money, if to hoard be thine;
But let thy daughter drink a younger wine!
Let her go rich and wise, in silk and fur;

Lay down a { bin that shall } grow old with her;
{ vintage to }

But thou, meantime, the while the batch is sound,
With pleased companions pass the bowl around;
Nor let the childless only taste delights,
For Fathers also may enjoy their nights.

IN CHARIDEMUM

YOU, Charidemus, who my cradle swung,
And watched me all the days that I was young;
You, at whose step the laziest slaves awake,
And both the bailiff and the butler quake;
The barber's suds now blacken with my beard,
And my rough kisses make the maids afeared;
But with reproach your awful eyebrows twitch,
And for the cane, I see, your fingers itch.
If something daintily attired I go,
Straight you exclaim: "Your father did not so."
And fuming, count the bottles on the board
As though my cellar were your private hoard.
Enough, at last: I have done all I can,
And your own mistress hails me for a man.

DE LIGURRA

YOU fear, Ligurra - above all, you long -
That I should smite you with a stinging song.
This dreadful honour you both fear and hope -
Both all in vain: you fall below my scope.
The Lybian lion tears the roaring bull,
He does not harm the midge along the pool.

Lo! if so close this stands in your regard,
From some blind tap fish forth a drunken barn,
Who shall with charcoal, on the privy wall,
Immortalise your name for once and all.

New Poems

IN LUPUM

BEYOND the gates thou gav'st a field to till;
I have a larger on my window-sill.
A farm, d'ye say? Is this a farm to you,
Where for all woods I spay one tuft of rue,
And that so rusty, and so small a thing,
One shrill cicada hides it with a wing;
Where one cucumber covers all the plain;
And where one serpent rings himself in vain
To enter wholly; and a single snail
Eats all and exit fasting to the pool?
Here shall my gardener be the dusty mole.
My only ploughman the . .. mole.
Here shall I wait in vain till figs be set,
And till the spring disclose the violet.
Through all my wilds a tameless mouse careers,
And in that narrow boundary appears,
Huge as the stalking lion of Algiers,
Huge as the fabled boar of Calydon.
And all my hay is at one swoop impresst
By one low-flying swallow for her nest,
Strip god Priapus of each attribute
Here finds he scarce a pedestal to foot.
The gathered harvest scarcely brims a spoon;
And all my vintage drips in a cocoon.
Generous are you, but I more generous still:
Take back your farm and stand me half a gill!

New Poems

AD QUINTILIANUM

O CHIEF director of the growing race,
Of Rome the glory and of Rome the grace,
Me, O Quintilian, may you not forgive
Before from labour I make haste to live?
Some burn to gather wealth, lay hands on rule,
Or with white statues fill the atrium full.
The talking hearth, the rafters sweet with smoke,
Live fountains and rough grass, my line invoke:
A sturdy slave, not too learned wife,
Nights filled with slumber, and a quiet life.

New Poems

DE HORTIS JULII MARTIALIS

MY Martial owns a garden, famed to please,
Beyond the glades of the Hesperides;
Along Janiculum lies the chosen block
Where the cool grottos trench the hanging rock.
The moderate summit, something plain and bare,
Tastes overhead of a serener air;
And while the clouds besiege the vales below,
Keeps the clear heaven and doth with sunshine glow.
To the June stars that circle in the skies
The dainty roofs of that tall villa rise.
Hence do the seven imperial hills appear;
And you may view the whole of Rome from here;
Beyond, the Alban and the Tuscan hills;
And the cool groves and the cool falling rills,
Rubre Fidenae, and with virgin blood
Anointed once Perenna's orchard wood.
Thence the Flaminian, the Salarian way,
Stretch far broad below the dome of day;
And lo! the traveller toiling towards his home;
And all unheard, the chariot speeds to Rome!
For here no whisper of the wheels; and tho'
The Mulvian Bridge, above the Tiber's flow,
Hangs all in sight, and down the sacred stream
The sliding barges vanish like a dream,
The seaman's shrilling pipe not enters here,
Nor the rude cries of porters on the pier.
And if so rare the house, how rarer far
The welcome and the weal that therein are!
So free the access, the doors so widely thrown,
You half imagine all to be your own.

AD MARTIALEM

GO(D) knows, my Martial, if we two could be
To enjoy our days set wholly free;
To the true life together bend our mind,
And take a furlough from the falser kind.
No rich saloon, nor palace of the great,
Nor suit at law should trouble our estate;
On no vainglorious statues should we look,
But of a walk, a talk, a little book,
Baths, wells and meads, and the veranda shade,
Let all our travels and our toils be made.
Now neither lives unto himself, alas!
And the good suns we see, that flash and pass
And perish; and the bell that knells them cries:
"Another gone: O when will ye arise? "

New Poems

IN MAXIMUM

WOULDST thou be free? I think it not, indeed;
But if thou wouldst, attend this simple rede:
When quite contented }thou canst dine at home
Thou shall be free when }
And drink a small wine of the march of Rome;
When thou canst see unmoved thy neighbour's plate,
And wear my threadbare toga in the gate;
When thou hast learned to love a small abode,
And not to choose a mistress A LA MODE:
When thus contained and bridled thou shalt be,
Then, Maximus, then first shalt thou be free.

AD OLUM

CALL me not rebel, though { here at every word
{in what I sing
If I no longer hail thee { King and Lord
{ Lord and King
I have redeemed myself with all I had,
And now possess my fortunes poor but glad.
With all I had I have redeemed myself,
And escaped at once from slavery and pelf.
The unruly wishes must a ruler take,
Our high desires do our low fortunes make:
Those only who desire palatial things
Do bear the fetters and the frowns of Kings;
Set free thy slave; thou settest free thyself.

New Poems

DE COENATIONE MICAE

LOOK round: You see a little supper room;
But from my window, lo! great Caesar's tomb!
And the great dead themselves, with jovial breath
Bid you be merry and remember death.

DE EROTIO PUELLA

THIS girl was sweeter than the song of swans,
And daintier than the lamb upon the lawns
Or Curine oyster. She, the flower of girls,
Outshone the light of Erythraean pearls;
The teeth of India that with polish glow,
The untouched lilies or the morning snow.
Her tresses did gold-dust outshine
And fair hair of women of the Rhine.
Compared to her the peacock seemed not fair,
The squirrel lively, or the phoenix rare;
Her on whose pyre the smoke still hovering waits;
Her whom the greedy and unequal fates
On the sixth dawning of her natal day,
My child-love and my playmate - snatcht away.

New Poems

AD PISCATOREM

FOR these are sacred fishes all
Who know that lord that is the lord of all;
Come to the brim and nose the friendly hand
That sways and can beshadow all the land.
Nor only so, but have their names, and come
When they are summoned by the Lord of Rome.
Here once his line an impious Lybian threw;
And as with tremulous reed his prey he drew,
Straight, the light failed him.
He groped, nor found the prey that he had ta'en.
Now as a warning to the fisher clan
Beside the lake he sits, a beggarman.
Thou, then, while still thine innocence is pure,
Flee swiftly, nor presume to set thy lure;
Respect these fishes, for their friends are great;
And in the waters empty all thy bait.